Cultural Studies in India: Diversity and Dynamics

Edited By

Dr. Mudasir Ahmad Gori

Prof. Mohammed Abdul Sami Siddiqui

Notion Press

Title: Cultural Studies in India: Diversity and Dynamics

Publisher: Notion Press
First published: 2024
Cover graphics: Canva, Open AI DALL-E-2
Concept and design: Dr. S M Fasiullah
MRP: 250/-

Contents

Preface

In today's diverse and globalized world, understanding culture is more crucial than ever. Culture shapes our identities, influences our beliefs, and impacts our interactions with others.

This book, titled *Cultural Studies in India: Diversity and Dynamics*, delves into the complex field of Cultural Studies within the Indian context, exploring the ways in which culture intersects with power, history, and identity.

Through a critical and interdisciplinary lens, the essays in this collection examine the ways in which culture is constructed, represented, and contested. They investigate how cultural practices and artifacts reflect and shape societal values, and how these social values can be used to challenge dominant narratives and promote social change.

This book is a journey into a complex terrain of Cultural Studies, inviting readers to engage with the theories, debates, and practices that shape our understanding of culture and its role in shaping our world. The essays attempt to provide a framework for understanding the dynamic interplay of traditions, emotions, popular culture, spirituality, and social structures in shaping human experiences. Indian culture, with its complexity and diversity, offers a compelling case study for examining these interactions.

By exploring themes such as moral ambiguity, social class, individualism and spirituality, the essays present the multifaceted nature of cultural identity and the ongoing negotiation between tradition and modernity.

This collection of essays would not have been possible without the efforts, support and patience of each and every author and contributor. We would like to thank everyone involved in making this book see the light of the day!

- *Editors*

Reverberations of Culture on Emotions

Dr. Nibha Thakore

Culture has a deep and far-reaching influence on an individual's emotional experience. The philosophical theories, spiritual knowledge, and ritual practices of a culture uphold profound significance. They have profound impressions of an individual's disposition and conduct. The paper attempts to delve into the constructive influences of cultural elements on the emotions of an individual. The paper studies numerous psychological theories to perceive the role of culture in governing emotions. The study aims to correlate theories and emotions while taking into consideration the Hindu culture._It inclines towards the Hindu culture in an endeavour to correlate the theories and emotions.

"Culture, or civilization taken in its widest ethnographic sense, is that complex whole which includes knowledge, belief, art, law, morals, custom, and any other capabilities and habits acquired by man as a member of society," stated Tylor in an attempt to engulf all the facets of culture. Though culture encompasses all the aspects of life, it mostly dominates our thoughts. Culture imparts a system of shared beliefs, a framework of set patterns of behaviour, and concurred norms thus shaping the emotional and mental constitution of an individual. This makes culture a psychological conjuncture. It has been only a few decades that mainstream psychology has acknowledged the significance of cultural influence on psychological processes and human behaviour. It makes the study of culture and its impact on human psychology imperative. The greatest challenge is to understand the link between cultural concepts at the community and the individual levels/1Psychology studied what goes on within individuals while culture deals with groups and societies at large. The only possible solution to the issue is the study of human emotions. To understand the influence of culture, we need to view the various traits of culture that influence emotions.

Emotion:

"An emotion is a complex psychological state that involves three distinct components: a subjective experience, a physiological response, and a behavioural or expressive response," remarked Hockenbury. Emotions are a response, and hence individual traits, moods, and the situation have a direct impact on it, making it a subjective experience. However, the culture and social construct to which an individual belongs also have a great influence on emotions. Averill provides a constructionist view of emotion, "...emotions are social constructions, not biologically given" (306). He calls emotions, syndromes which are constituted by social norms which are further represented psychologically as cognitive structures. He further explains that these structures "provide the basis for an appraisal for stimuli, the organization of responses, and the monitoring of behaviour, that is, for the improvisation of emotional roles" (306). Cognition evaluates the social stimuli and responses concerning the social norms. Emotions are interpretations rooted in a social context as well as within the cognitive structures or schemata of an individual. Michelle Rosaldo contends "Feelings are not substances to be discovered in our blood but social practices organized by stories that we enact and tell. They are structured by our forms of understanding" (143). Culture, thus, moulds our minds and governs our perception which is reflected in our emotional reactions.

Emotions are a universal phenomenon. Darwin in his theory proposes that emotional expressions are evolved, adaptive, and are outer manifestations of the inner state of an individual. Providing the example of laughter, Darwin points out those certain emotional expressions are the outcome of the need of the nervous system to discharge excess excitement. In his frequently cited theory, Darwin recognizes the communicative function of emotion expression, "We have also seen that expression in itself, or the language of the emotions, as it has sometimes been called, is certainly of importance for the welfare of mankind" (366). Researchers have contradictory views about the expression of specific emotions as universal or similar in various cultures and that the expressions vary from culture to culture. Culture provides norms, structure, and yardsticks to interpret and express emotions. Illouz et al. state, "Culture provides the framework for the labeling, classification, categorization, and interpretation of emotions, and social norms regulate and form their expression and even their experience" (221). Culture develops standards to regulate and display emotions, which are generally gender-based. Some cultures encourage the expression of emotions, while in other cultures, "suppressing one's emotions to better fit in with the emotions of the group is looked at as mature and appropriate" (Bagheri et al.125).

The study of emotions in the context of human psychology and culture would help us realize the deep-rooted meanings of the cultural bearings.

Happiness:

R. Veenhoven defines happiness as, "the overall appreciation of one's life as-a-whole" and further states that happiness is synonymous with 'life satisfaction' and 'subjective well-being." (452). Veenhoven (2006) identifies four qualities of life which represent happiness - livability of the environment, life-ability of the person, the utility of life, and satisfaction with life. The livability of the environment means the quality of life; life ability refers to the ability of an individual to cope with the problems of life; the utility of life points to leading a useful life and satisfaction with life deals with the appreciation of life (3-4).

The Hindu culture divides life into four stages – *brahmacharya ashram, grihastha ashram, vanprastha ashram,* and *sanyas ashram* – with a specially assigned role for each individual. The *brahmacharya ashram* imparts education and life learning skills to the individual. Chanakya suggested that while a student is learning, he should give up on any comfort or happiness. In the second stage, *grahasth ashram*, an individual is allowed to indulge in worldly pleasures guided by dharma or duty. In the next stage- *vanprastha ashram* the individual becomes a forest dweller and focuses on spirituality and in the last stage *sanyas ashram*, the individual becomes a *sanyasi* or monk and renounces everything to pursue self-realization. Nelson et al. state that "According to need satisfaction and goal theories pursuing goals and satisfying needs result in happiness" (251). The division of life in stages constitutes a perfect life, encompassing every aspect of life – emotional, economic, religious, spiritual, and philosophical. An experience of all the facets provides the individual with life satisfaction. When an individual achieves goals defined in each stage of life, he or she finds peace and happiness. There is rare adherence to the concept but the ideology behind the stages still has an influence.

Hindu worldview states that all attachment (*māyā*) is an illusion and a source of all human misery. Thus, Indian psychology emphasizes detachment from all worldly pleasures. The Bhagvad Gita offers the idea of a *sthitaprajna* person, the one who has his senses under control and neither gets attached to pleasant ideas nor gets frustrated by negative outcomes. Such an individual is at peace as he strives for self-realization and is spiritually inclined. Only a peaceful individual is a happy individual. Dharm Bhawok states, "Happiness is presented as the consequent of peace, and just like a person pursuing desires is said to never achieve peace, a person who is not at peace is said to be ever unhappy. Thus the first path to peace presented in *Bhagavad Gita* is captured in the term *Kamasa Mkalpavivarjana* or shedding desires, which is the prerequisite of happiness." (130-131).

Csikszentmihalyi (1991) came up with the term 'flow' in which "action follows upon action according to an internal logic that seems to not need conscious intervention by the actor" (36). When this flow of repeated activities becomes autotelic, it provides enjoyment. The concept is well applicable to the rituals of devotion in Indian culture. Singing *bhajans*, clapping, collective dancing, chanting the name of God are forms of worship that can be termed as the flow experience. Csikszentmihalyi (1991) states, that "people in flow report a *loss of self-consciousness*" (185). It is a universal observation of believers during the act of devotion or worship. Paranjpe states that in Hindu culture "the joy derived from singing, dancing, and similar artistic expressions of devotion has been considered similar to, but not the same as, the ultimate bliss (*brahmānanda*)" (295).

Terror:

The terror management theory proposed by Greenberg et al. states that an individual faces two major terrors in his life – the terror of being alone and the dread of mortality. This is where the individual turns to culture which provides him the assurance of togetherness and the possibility of immortality. Being part of a cultural group frees man from the fear of being alone. An individual strives to be good, helpful, and valuable to gain acceptance and to avoid being abandoned. He/ she struggles to live up to the standards of the cultural demands. Culture provides a sense of esteem that caters to the needs of humans to view them as valuable. Culture projects the world as meaningful, orderly, and permanent and thus imparts a sense of value to an individual as a member of the culture. The acceptance and affection an individual receives from the co-members of the culture is a very important source of a sense of personal value (Greenberg et al., 202).

The Hindu culture values togetherness and harmony in relations. Interpersonal connectedness with family, friends, and neighbors is nurtured. It emphasizes celebrations; apart from the celebration of important events in life such as birth and weddings, there is an abundance of annual festivals and weekly congregations. Festivals usually have a specific fun activity, while songs, dance, decorations, costumes, and food are the regular rudiments in all celebrations. Gathering people and engaging in positive activities, in turn, generates positive emotions.

Human beings crave immortality; with literal immortality being unattainable, they are satisfied with a symbolic form of perpetuity. In Ernest Becker's words, "This is the terror: to have emerged from nothing, to have a name, consciousness of self, deep inner feelings, an excruciating inner yearning for life and self-expression – and with all this yet to die" (Becker, 1973, p. 87). Culture teaches how to live a meaningful life and helps to deal with the questions of existence. Kesebir observes, "The opportunities presented by religion to interact with the sacred; to transcend one's mundane, creaturely existence; and to get in touch with something from the realm of immortality might thus engender jolts of meaning for the individual, thereby helping to ease death anxiety" (8).

Every culture propounds the concept of the continuation of life in a different manner. It offers a favorable viewpoint that denies the ultimate vulnerability and morality of man (Greenberg et al., 196). The idea within the culture is that there is a definite system of life and death and that there is a possibility of immortality that assures an individual, reduces fear, and motivates to have a deep and indubitable faith in the culture. Greenberg et al. state, "Culture reduces the terror endangered by awareness of our vulnerability and mortality by providing a shared symbolic conception of reality that imputes order, predictability, significance, and permanence to our lives" (206).

In Hinduism, the concept of death is a disappearance of what previously existed. The aatima or consciousness cannot die. The objectified consciousness or the physical body is destroyed which is nothing but a change of individual consciousness. The Hindu culture propagates the idea of rebirth and terms death as a stage in spiritual evolution. *Mokshā* means a release from the consequences of actions (*kārma*) and liberation from the never-ending cycle of rebirth. It is the attainment of supreme immortal bliss and hence the ultimate goal of life. In every life, an individual should free himself from worldly entanglements to achieve this singular truth.

Culture employs a variety of mechanisms to provide a solution to the question of mortality. Symbolic immortality can be achieved by being a part of a larger entity such as culture, ethnicity, or religion. Becker mentions that being part of something substantial, "gives him a sense of self-expansion in a larger beyond, and so heightens his being, giving him truly a feeling of transcendent value" (1973,152). Culture endorses that symbolic immortality can be gained by a significant achievement, which will last beyond the lifespan of an individual. Acts of great importance elevate the value of the individual and magnify his existence. Another mechanism is to continue the name of the individual through progeny.

Stress:

Stress is an individual's reaction to a physical, emotional, or social challenge. Lazarus (1984) defined stress as, "a relationship between the person and the environment that is appraised as taxing or exceeding his or her resources and endangering his or her well-being" (21). Aldwin presents a four-point relationship between stress and culture - first, the cultural contexts define the stress an individual is likely to face; second, culture has an impact on the appraisal of stressfulness; third, the method of choosing a solution has a cultural influence and lastly culture provides solutions to eliminate stress (565). Certain cultural norms and practices that dominate life events generate stress, such as a wedding or retirement. There are factors within the culture that aggravate stress levels of individuals, hence Arsenian and Arsenian bifurcated culture as tough and easy (377). A tough culture would be the one that offers a few valued goals to an individual and limited means to achieve those goals, while the easy culture proposed multiple-valued goals and motivational constructs and relatively easy and more means to achieve them.

The laws, beliefs, and norms in culture are structured in such a way that they administer advice and solutions to problems. The Hindu culture offers a range of coping resources and mechanisms from philosophical doctrines of fate to physical workouts of yoga. The Karma theory emphasizes the inescapability of one's actions of the past lives and the present.

The inevitability of the consequences of actions resulting in pain and pleasure is beyond an individual's clasp. Robert Biswas-Diener mentions, "… Indians feel life is a series of fated circumstances rather than under immediate and direct personal control…" (21) This philosophy of fate paradoxically helps an individual to not stress out unnecessarily. Certain prescribed activities boost optimism and serenity such as meditation, prayer, and charity. The cultural activities and their divine meanings generate a sense of belonging and the submergence of the self into the cosmos which provides an individual the strength to face the misfortunes of the world.

Calmness:

Rituals are repeated activities that have a symbolic meaning and are passed down from one generation to the next. The rituals are believed to have cosmic powers to produce a magical effect - from a shower of rain to the birth of a child. The Hindu culture has rituals and chants for every occasion, be it communicating with the unborn (*gārbhsānskar*) or offering food to the dead (*shraddh*). The commitment to continue the rituals lends it a sense of responsibility and significance. Cultural symbols objectify the culture making it easy to create a connection. Faith can be sustained on objects and solid things that can be seen. The social acceptance of the symbols and the historical adherence of rituals by our ancestors lend them a unique prominence. The most ordinary actions or set of behavior offer a chance to express emotions and bring about a sense of calmness.

Rituals provide organization to the family and social life, give a sense of stability during tough times, and have a therapeutic impact on individuals. Hobson et al. state that rituals "impose order against threatening forces of chaos and disorder" (5). Hobson et al. delineate a framework of ritual processing, the bottom-up and the top-down. The bottom-up framework suggests that performing rituals distract an individual from emotional turmoil. Hobson et al. state, "Rituals then can serve as a form of distraction, blocking out possible negative thoughts from entering a person's mind" (6). Another bottom-up mechanism states that the successful completion of a sequence of rituals regulates the emotions and provides a sense of stability, "…the motoric rigidity of ritual actions satisfies a fundamental need for order, and may help to regulate emotions especially in response to anxious events" (Hobson et al., 6). The top-down processing continues with the idea and adds that the inherent meaning in the rituals helps in gaining control over the self. "Participating in a religious ritual provides people with a sense of comfort, because doing the practice reminds them that they belong to something bigger than themselves" (Hobson et al., p 7).

Belonging:

Family rituals provide a sense of belonging to the members as following the ritual requires coordination among the members. The behavior of all family members is uniform while performing a ritual. This synchronization of behaviour connects the individuals, helps them share emotions, and strengthens the family ties. In a time when everyone is busy with their work, punctuality rituals lend a sense of cohesiveness to the lives of other family members. For carrying out a family ritual all the members of the family have to plan their schedule accordingly. Reiss gives the example of having dinner together at six every evening which requires everyone to plan their daily activities before and after the scheduled dinner at six. The outcome of the ritual in the words of Reiss is, "... planning and punctuality rituals give each family member a special sense of synchrony with, if not embroilment in, each other's lives" (242).

Ceremonies foster an individual's identity as a part of a cultural group and aid in bonding with a similar cultural group. Reiss mentions, "The formal features of ceremonials contribute to the temporary surrender of the individual to a sense of merger with the group." (pg 244) Ceremonies, especially the religious ones, charge the atmosphere with positive vibes which lends a sense of calm to an individual. The rituals performed during the ceremonies have a greater symbolic meaning. While participating in a ceremony, the focus on the rituals and the grasp of the positive aura shift the issues to the background. In Hinduism, birth rituals, death rites, and wedding ceremonies are designed to benefit the individuals concerned as well as the people around.

Loss:

Rando observed that performing a ritual provided a sense of control in an otherwise uncontrollable event of losing a loved one. Romanoff's model presented the concept of three functions of rituals – continuation of connection with the lost loved one, transition to the new social role, and change of sense of self to adapt to the changed relationship with the lost one. Doka mentions the functions as asserting a continuing bond with the deceased, noting transformations in the grief journey, confirming the legacy of the lost one, and encouraging a symbolic reconciliation with him/her. Van der Hart and Ebbers focus on bidding goodbye to the past and Kastenbaum considers these a starting point of recovery and renewal.

The main purpose of the mourning ritual in Hinduism is to make the grievers accept the death and express and process their grief. The venting out of grief helps lower the levels of sorrow and make people emotionally stable. In Rajasthan and Punjab, professional mourners (*rudali*) are hired to mourn extravagantly by wailing, singing mourning songs, or dancing so that the family can alleviate their sorrow under their influence. The mourning rituals are designed in a way that aids restoration of control over the emotions and accepts the reality of loss. Rituals are a set of defined actions and help people in situation where they don't understand what to do. Performing a ritual creates a calm atmosphere that gives individuals space to reorganize their thoughts and emotions and deal with the loss. The custom of organizing readings of Bhagavad Gita, hymns, and chanting brings clarity and positivity to thoughts. Rituals and ceremonies are spread over days so that the family of the deceased can get the support of friends and relatives. The planning of the events too helps the family members take their minds off the loss.

Emotions play a critical role in our lives, from guiding our behaviour and experiences to making and breaking relationships. A basic understanding of the cultural influences on emotions can help us understand our behaviour and attitude. The positive impact of culture on our emotions and mental constitution helps us value our culture and realize the deeper and hidden meanings of cultural norms and customs. The view that the role of culture is constructive and regulative would aid in solving many problems and predicaments.

Cultural tradition and philosophical terrain in Hinduism are based on profound psychological insights. The ancient ancestors looked for explanations of cause and effect in an unscientific world. The wise makers of culture have provided a solution to every perceivable problem which depicts their deep understanding of human troubles, human behaviour, reaction, instincts, and emotional turmoil. There is a concern for searching for ways to cure human suffering and the result is an elaborate coping mechanisms. Indian philosophy and rituals are designed to manage emotions and to provide order to chaos.

References:

Aldwin, Carolyn M. "Culture, coping and resilience to stress." Gross National Happiness and Development - Proceedings of the First International Conference on Operationalization of Gross National Happiness. Centre for Bhutan Studies, pp. 563-573, 2004.

Arsenian, John & M. Arsenian. "Tough and Easy Cultures: A Conceptual Analysis." *Psychiatry*, Vol. 11, No. 4, Pp.377-385, 1948.

Averill, J. R. "A Constructionist View of Emotion." *Emotion: Theory, Research, and Experience*. Edited by R. Plutchik& H. Kellerman, Academic Press, Vol.1, Pp.305- 339, 1980.

Bagheri, Z., A. Kosnin, and M. Besharat. "The Influence of Culture on the Functioning of Emotional Intelligence." Published in proceedings of 2nd International Seminar on Quality and Affordable Education, Pp. 123-127, 2013.

Bhawuk, Dharm. *Spirituality and Indian Psychology: Lessons from the Bhagavad-Gita*. Springer, 2011.

Popular Culture: A Perspective and Cultural Crossovers

Aadil Zeffer

Popular culture is a set of objects, beliefs, or practices that represent the commonly shared meanings of a social system such as fashion, entertainment, trends, leisure, linguistic conventions, and media objects, etc. Popular culture is the 'culture of the people shaped by how people engage in their daily lives, dressing patterns, greeting habits, interactions between people, use of slang, food habits, and everyday activities etc. It incorporates the most immediate and existing aspects of our lives which are subject to frequent changes, particularly in the present technological times where the omnipresent media brings people closer. It serves an egalitarian and inclusive role in society in uniting the masses around values, belongingness, and a sense of identity. Furthermore, in popular culture, we always have a scope to change the prevailing or dominant norms of behaviour which is otherwise difficult in folk or high culture. Since there is a high scope of crossovers, people are drawn to popular culture. This provides them to experience both individual satisfaction and community bonding.

Culture can be simply described as 'a particular way of life' and includes activities, behaviours, beliefs, traditions, norms, rituals, values, and the like. Culture is prominently associated with ethnic or national groups, for instance, African culture, American culture, Indian culture, Japanese culture, and so on. Yet, the term 'culture' can also be applied to discuss cultures based on age, generation, gender, work, profession, tastes, etc. For example, in age groups, we can see cultures like-children's culture, youth culture, and senior culture; in generation-Generation X culture, Baby Boomer culture and Millennial culture; in gender- male culture, female culture, transgender culture; in organizations - McDonald's culture, Starbucks culture, and Microsoft culture; in professions - doctors culture, police officers culture, and so on. The concept of culture can further be applied to one's interests or tastes such as casino culture, cricket culture, discotheques culture, glamour culture, hip-hop culture, pub culture, film and entertainment culture, adventurous culture, restaurant culture, and most importantly Popular Cultures. In his book, *Culture and Society*, Raymond Williams states that the idea of culture came during the period of the Industrial Revolution and subsequently the word 'culture' changed its meaning. First, it came to mean, 'a general state or habit of mind'. Second, 'the general state of intellectual development, in a society as a whole. Third, 'the general body of the arts' and fourth, it came to mean 'a whole way of life, intellectual, material and spiritual'(xvi).

Popular Culture: A Perspective:

There have been various debates regarding the common forms of culture and the shifting understanding of popular culture. The meanings of 'popular culture' depend on the context of use and who defines it. It is widely understood as the people's culture that is prevalent in a society at a given time. It includes the areas of social life that the public is most actively interested in and involved. It reflects widely held beliefs, ideals, values, and standards. Under its universality, it represents influences, and shapes the day-to-day lives of people. So, we can say that popular culture is a mode of identity or expression of a specific society at a particular point in time. It consists of the aspects of attitudes, behaviours, beliefs, customs, traditions, languages, and tastes that define the people of any society. (Wagner 48). The culture of one place may be differentiated from the popular culture of other places. The recent commentary about culture is that there is nothing like the pre-existing common culture of the people that can serve as a ground for an administration or a state to develop. In its traditional sense, it refers to the culture of people, allowing them to identify collectively. Popular culture is perceived as a set of activities by a kind of culture makers or artists that result in performances, received, and interpreted by audiences.

Folk culture and High culture are generally differentiated from Popular culture. Folk culture generally represents the traditional way of doing things, discourages innovation and radical creativity, and is less adaptable to change. It is local in orientation and more stable than a popular culture which is always on the lookout for something new and exciting. An important feature of popular culture is that it is accessible to the general public whereas high culture is not intended for mass consumption. In this way, popular culture is mass-marketed and mass-produced on a large societal scale. On the other hand, Folk culture (folklore, folk art, folk crafts, and folk music) is produced, distributed, and usually emanates from local or regional groups of people.

The concept of high culture such as ballet, theatre, classical works, classical music, opera, art museums, etc. is associated with the social elite or the upper socioeconomic classes which necessitates extensive training and preparation. Popular culture includes cultural texts, graffiti, Hollywood films, rock music, and working-class practices, produced and consumed on a mass scale. It is important to note that sometimes even the common masses participate in high culture and similarly social elites in popular culture.

There are three other, similar subsets of culture which are worth discussing. Let's take subculture as the first one. It is a culture within a culture and focuses on ethnicity/race, etc. For example, in American culture, there is Indian-American culture, African-American culture and so on which are subcultures of a broad and overarching American Culture. Similarly, subcultures within mainstream music can be described as hip hop culture, rock culture, and so on. Again, the 'Southern' culture within the USA is different from the 'East Coast' culture, in which people have their own way of talking and doing things, etc. Nonetheless, both are a part of the larger U.S. culture and the American Dream. etc. A related concept is a counterculture that describes itself in opposition to another culture. For example, the feminist movement stands against gender inequality. Another mode of culture is co-culture, existing alongside the dominant or mainstream culture within a society. For example, Latino culture exists alongside White culture as a co-culture in the United States.

Popular Culture: Influences and Formation:

According to social anthropologist Ernest Gellner, the social meaning of culture is highly contextual and local. It is only eighteenth century onwards that we see the appearance of the notion of culture as a shared atmosphere such as a common set of beliefs, customs, and languages. He further argues that the origins of this common national culture in industrial modernity are not from ordinary folk but from the centralised authority of the state and its educational apparatus (10). Throughout history, humans have been influenced and dominated by customs and traditions determined by local folk culture. It is concluded that before the eighteenth century the conditions were not found favourable for the growth of 'popular culture' as the majority of people concentrated around small areas.

During the onset of the Industrial era, people from rural areas started to move towards cities, resulting in the Urbanisation of the West. All this played a significant role in the development of Popular culture. People now found themselves within a wide range of cultural influences and diversity in contrast to their earlier homogeneous village experience. Now, this mixed lot of people from diverse backgrounds would come to see themselves as a 'collective unit' in popular forms of expression. Many historians and scholars are of the view that the rise of the middle class brought by the Industrial Revolution is the main reason for the advent of popular culture. We can observe that this industrialization brought in a multitude of new things like advancements in architecture and buildings, mass production, a substantial increase in literacy rate, developments in transportation, improved public health facilities, and the development of printing and mass media in general, etc. All these factors contributed greatly to the growth of popular culture.

At the beginning of the twentieth century, we witness the mass production of newspapers, serialized novels, stories, and periodicals which became sources of reliable information for the general public, who were becoming interested in social and economic issues. The ideas presented in print served as a springboard for public debate and popular discourse on a wide range of topics which was fuelled further by technological growth. Throughout the twentieth century, the advent of new forms of mass media greatly impacted popular culture. Cinema radio and television all had a profound influence on popular culture.

Through the late 1700s, the above-cited factors such as technological advancement, industrialization, urbanization, and mass media played a major role in the formation of popular culture in the western world. These continue to shape popular culture today as well. In addition to offering a common ground for the masses, the urban culture inspires ideals of individualistic aspirations, wherein there are no limitations to what an individual wants to accomplish. In such a society, founded on the premise of individual rights, the individuals or the masses partake in all that is 'popular' or they may choose an action that is unfrequented and off the beaten track. Sometimes such unique styles are easily adopted by others, and it ceases to become uncommon and unfrequented, it grows and becomes, popular. So, sometimes such 'pathfinders' play a key role in affecting the popular culture by their individuality.

Classical sociologists broadly spoke about the concept and role of culture in shaping human social life. The Birmingham and Frankfurt Schools of thought promoted an interdisciplinary analysis of popular culture that included a spectrum of sociological insights. As previously said, popular culture comes from a variety of sources, the primary being the mass media which includes television, music, books, films, radio, and most importantly the internet. Such advancements allow greater transmission of ideas. This mash-up of popular culture sources represents an innovative way of piquing the interest of the public. Professional institutions such as news channels, publishing houses, and expert opinion that provide information to the public often affect Popular culture. They influence and shape the collective opinion of the public on a particular subject and offer a platform for public discourse and democratic dialogue. Thus, the analysis of culture is inextricably related to the study of economics, politics, and society. There is a lot of scope for pluralism, multiplicity, and openness to difference and marginalised voices in this new world order of technology, where the globalization of media provides the public access channels.

Culture: Cultural Crossovers:

By Culture, we mean the environment in which different organisms grow as well as the process of growth itself. Over the last two centuries, the study of culture has been shaped by various disciplines like sociology, anthropology, philosophy, arts, history, media studies, linguistics, politics, history, psychoanalysis etc. Cultural Studies has been influenced by these surrounding disciplines which have 'culture' as their object of analysis. As a field, Cultural Studies is disciplined through its focus on certain kinds of methodology and cultural theory. Cultural studies have become a common site for thinking across disciplinary spaces in a variety of ways. Furthermore, it provides a framework for considering the cross-overs across disciplines and fields of research.

The crossovers of popular culture are too many and include a wide array of genres such as cyber-culture, entertainment, popular music, sports, print, leisure, advertising, fads, and television, etc. The most widely consumed examples of popular culture are the Internet, sports, and technology. These also represent its great staying power. People from all walks of life enjoy being associated with sports in any form, watch long hours of television, and show their allegiance to internet browsing. The world community as a whole consumes these things which play a key role in people's lives. In the present scenario, one feels difficult to imagine a world without popular culture.

The recent developments, innovations, and cross-overs within the arts, humanities and social sciences and physical and medical sciences have played an important role in the formation of cultural studies. The research relations among texts, the film culture for mapping the physical connections between different identities in geographical space, the space for thinking about the economics of globalization and the processes or the imaginings have a say about the nature of culture. In this sense, we can say that cultural studies is a place, where it is possible to analyze the relations across the natural and artificial, human and non-human or the technological and the organic, questioning the conventional understanding of the divisions between culture and materiality, culture and nature or culture and technology. It is also a fact that some fields have dominated the production and shaping of cultural meanings, identities, and institutions of power.

In its relatively short history as a discipline, Cultural Studies has been mainly concerned with popular culture: which carries the connotations of ordinariness rather than elatedness, of entertainment rather than high art, of commercialism rather than community, and standardization rather than individuality. The valorisation of popular culture as an anthropological or sociological phenomenon has sparked a lot of interest. Some of us may see culture as a simple phenomenon but the academic investigation indicates the complexity of the phenomenon. In many texts, it is found that popular culture does not have any fixed definition. Raymond Williams identifies five perspectives on popular culture: a notion which is made through the craftwork of people, a notion that it is framed within a structural relation of power between the ruling class and the people, and understanding that it is a marker of bad taste within the field of cultural distinction, a notion that it is popular in quantitative terms and a notion which is used as a means of ideological persuasion. People form the basic foundation and pre-exist any social formation of a culture or society but for some, the idea of the people is a product of a society that survives within its ideological context. Their unities in terms of common culture or language form the natural bedrock.

Thus the correlations across people and society are important in the realm of culture which is studied through the contours and dynamics of modernity and history. In the historical context, people were differentiated along the lines of competition and approached differently. For example in the eighteenth or nineteenth centuries, the composition of people formed mostly the industrial working class. In the centuries that followed the advent of the concept of democracy led to a questioning of social position, citizenship and class. In the twenty-first century, there was a further reordering of people in the wake of post-modernization, post-industrialization, and globalization.

This gives us an idea about how the popularity of culture works and how it changes trends over some time, what its relations are and who controls it. Under these factors, we can say that Cultural theory calls into question the common sense understanding of the term 'popular culture' and undermines any stable notion of 'the people' as an entity. There are several more questions that can be raised here such as; Does popular culture exist in fleeting moments or is it an everyday phenomenon? Does it also decline as a consequence of a changing environment or of the growing significance of new technological innovations? It is ironic that at a moment when 'popular culture' started to become a legitimate area of academic study, its foundation in wider social and political realities began to crumble.

Culture is not merely the adornment and legitimation of social order, but rather a necessarily shared medium. The members of the society can breathe, speak, produce and survive within culture alone because it is perhaps the minimal shared atmosphere or the life-blood. In the present era, the rise of forms of new knowledge and productive technologies facilitates the mass production of products (Aglietta, 79). As a discipline, Cultural Studies continuously shifts its interests and methods due to its constant interaction with larger historical context. The mappings and struggles of the nation-state form our understanding of culture. We can see this concern of 'culture' and 'civilization' in the development of nations on tracing their histories. In the present context, the concepts like consumer culture, globalization, new technologies, and multiculturalism have raised questions and doubts about the appropriateness of the term 'popular culture'

References:

Adorno, Theodor. *The Culture Industry*. London: Routledge, 1991.

Aglietta, Michel. *A Theory of Capitalist Regulation*. London: Verso, 1979.

Arnold, Matthew. *Culture and Anarchy*. London: Cambridge UP, 1960.

Burnett, R. *Postmodern image communities in Cultures of Vision: Images, Media and the Imaginary.* Bloomington: Indiana University Press. 1995.

Gellner, Ernest. *Nations and Nationalism.* Oxford: Blackwell, 1983.

Wagner, Peter. *Theorizing Modernity.* London: Sage, 2001.

Wagner, Peter. *A History and Theory of the Social Sciences.* London: Sage, 2001.

Reflection and Exploration of Indian Culture: A Study of Select Indian Films

Dr. Gulab K Shaikh

The present research paper analyses the reflection of Indian culture as well as its manifestation through films. It also highlights select Indian Bollywood films which have successfully explored the sensibilities of Indian culture. Culture is the evidence of people's personal, professional and artistic life. Culture embodies elements of knowledge, arts beliefs, myths, rituals, education, architecture, customs, habits, regular practices, manners, and perceptions of any geographical land. Indian creative films beyond the object of entertainment have successfully conveyed the cultural patterns of colonial and post-colonial phases effectually. The sensational and unexplored issues of culture are presented through films that enhanced the consciousness of people.

Indian cinema is recognized as the most influential medium of addressing several socio-culture issues successfully. Since its derivation, Indian cinema has been persuasively communicating cultural messages on screens. Beyond the vital component of entertainment, Indian films have become the seminal elements of Indian Culture. The Hindi film industry and regional industries have been producing remarkable films that have received recognition and appeal from people. Various genres of film such as horror, comedy, thriller and romance have enriched the glory of great Indian films. The assortment of subjects, themes, and ideas as well as the embodiment of social values in film has created an impressive image of Indian cinema amongst audiences. Gabe Moura has aptly commented on the significance and importance of cinema in the following words: Since the days of its inception, cinema has been one of the important tools of expression of ideas. It is a miniature of the societal values and prevailing trends of society. A source of ideas and values, it has served as a carrier of transformation and revolution. It provides a platform where society can crave introspection for a positive change. (Moura)

The creative movies of Bollywood follow a dissimilar pathway from mainstream cinema because the component of creative movies extensively differs from established films. The scarcity of creative films in Bollywood is noticeable for the fear of **a** less audience and profit. The creative film is a powerful medium across the world in raising socio-cultural and political issues. Moreover, gender inequality, dowry, caste discrimination, female foeticide, and mental disorder have been effectively brought on screen by Indian creative films. Films are a mirror of society, they explore the dimensions of existing culture effectively but the success of creative films is often uncertain. It is largely observed that cinema positively brings socio-cultural changes in society. Some directors and producers have profoundly taken efforts to explore the culture of India. Cinema is a composite art form embodying visuals, sounds, colours, and music that appeal to the audience extensively.

Hypotheses and Methodology:

The present research work explores the significant role of films in the reflection of Indian culture and sensibilities. The researcher attempted an analytical method to study the selected problem. The research problem is based on the following hypotheses.

1. Experimental cinema explores realistic elements effectively.
2. Creative and artistic films attempt to explore the chosen concept comprehensively.
3. Films on partition, history, and destruction explore the contemporary cultural dimensions of the concerned phase.
4. Films are an evident part of life. Beyond entertainment, they have been performing the role of a social weapon.

Scope and Limitations of Study:

Though there is extensive research on films and films studies under different perspectives, yet the present study attempts a significant effort to explore the reflection of Indian culture in select Bollywood films. The research problem has scope for further study. The present study deals with select five films and slightly touches on other films. The study highlights the notion that films are an effective medium of exploration and reflection of the culture that presents a sensible portrait of the concerned phase comprehensively.

Study of the Problem:

The Indian film industry is the world's leading industry producing around 800 to 1000 films in a year which are about twofold to Hollywood films. Bollywood shares a major split in Indian cinema with its headquarters in Mumbai and the embodiment of an uncountable amount. Since the film *Raja Harishchandra,* Indian cinema has witnessed frequent changes. The diverse forms of Indian films help convey the social attitudes, manners, cultural transformation, cultural encounters, and changing perceptions of society. Films perform the role of entertainment and at the same time communicate awareness and consciousness with moral messagess. Cultural and social awareness through various experiments is the hallmark of Indian cinema. The films are theme-oriented and when a director and producer produce a film representing a historical era, historical event, or any crucial event at that time, the film automatically embodies the elements of culture.

On the other hand, India is a territory of diverse cultures. The tradition of long-entrenched culture in India is still persistent. Languages, customs, manners clothing habits and household activity of every geographic part in India differ and vary in forms. The cultural condition of India in the Muslim phase and colonized phase under the British has also been portrayed in various films. There are several films like *Border*, *Mangal Pande*, *Bhagat Singh*, *Netaji Subhash Chandra Bose,* and *M.K. Gandhi* exploring the culture of colonization and patriotism. Films like *Train to Pakistan* neatly describe the condition and culture of patriotism. In a way, an Indian film explores the canvas of every cultural phase and tries to unveil the cultural dimensions of each phase. The films *Mughal-e-Azam*, *Taare Zameen Par*, *Lagaan, Rang De Basanti,* and *My Brother Nikhil* are selected for the present study to validate and explore the chosen problem.

Mughal-e-Azam: A Retrospection of Indian Diversified Culture (1960)

This film is a celebrated milestone of Indian cinema that arrived on screen in 1960. This film was inspired by a play Anarkali written by Imtiaz Ali in 1922 and rewritten in 1931. This film comprehensively explores the contemporary Mughal culture and especially Islamic culture. The renowned author Rachel Dwyer in her book *Filming the Gods: Religion and Indian Cinema* remarks about the exceptional features of the films as:

"The film highlights religious tolerance between Hindus and Muslims. The example includes the scenes of Hindu queen Jodhabai's presence in the court of the Muslim Akbar, the singing of Hindu devotional song by Anarkali, and Akbar's participation in the Janmashtami celebrations, during which

Akbar is shown pulling a string to rock a swing with an idol of Krishna on it."

The film allegorically presents history and heritage by emphasizing national identity. Different cultures and personal and professional lives and culture of all characters such as prince Salim, Anarkali, and other courtesans have precisely been explored in the film. The culture of palaces, kings, queens, romance, love, administration, and conspiracies is effectively explored through characters and events. The practice of aesthetic poetic language for communication is also crystallized in the film. The cultural conflict of love and resistance from family members as well as the struggle of royals between duty and desires has been extensively shown in the film.

From realistic perception, the film conveys to us an era of palaces and battles. The contemporary historical reality and existing culture of people has been documented in the film. Mughal empire, administration, and existing Mughal culture is the prime background of the film. The film is timeless because it has captured all opulence of aesthetics. The social evils and bitter realities of the contemporary time are still prevalent in sub-continents portrayed in the film. The characters, dialogues, and actions of the movie reflect a strong sense of tradition and people. The song *pyar kiya to darna kya* effectively exposes the culture of romance and passionate bond between two lovers. The dress and jewellery apparelled by the characters in the film reflect the richness and culture of **a** palace. The battle of soldiers focuses on the culture of war. The Hindu Muslim bonding and tolerance of culture is effectively explored in the film. It is a milestone in Indian cinema with its multiple salient futures and embodying strong elements of contemporary culture.

Rang De Basanti: Emergence of Ignited Youths (2000)

This film was released on Republic Day 26-January 2006 and preciously explores the feeling of transparency and devotion amongst youth. The title of the film itself manifests the feeling of devotion and renaissance among youth. The film describes a group of Indian youth and a foreign woman engaged in theatrical activities. It is a fine explanation of history with modern topography. At the outset, the film seems a typical of Bollywood but an incident in the life of the characters changes the plot and life of all the leading characters in the movie. A dear friend of the leading characters and a lieutenant in the Indian Air Force dies in a plane crash. The youngsters in the movie demand justice for the death of their friend but the government pays no serious consideration towards their demand.

The protagonists decide to protest against the unreceptive response of the government and demand the resignation of the Defence Minister. The film symbolizes various sheds of contemporary culture. Corruption, mismanagement, lack of coordination, and feeling of the dominance of government culture are symbolized in the film. The bonding of Hindus and Muslims despite several conflicts has been explored in the films.

The culture of generation gap bridging this through education and common sense has efficiently been shown in the movie. More importantly, the film personifies the youth culture of India and exposes the feeling and awareness aroused among youth. It is also observed that the youth of India is more conscious about their rights of protest and justice. The creative force of youth reflected through their theatrical activities and the sense of opposing the wrong standing against injustice, appreciating the right, working for better are some of the salient features of Indian youth culture documented in the film.

Taare Zameen Par: New Trend of Gaze (2007)

This film was written by Amol Gupte and Deepa Bhatia and directed by Aamir Khan. It is observed that children born in contemporary times are surrounded by various medical health issues. Moreover, the approach of parents towards children is no less than winning the race. A child is treated as a machine product to earn the decided target. *Taare Zameen Par* explores the story of an eight year old dyslexic child. The movie successfully brings out the trauma of the child who is suppressed under the collision of society, family, and school. The central character of the movie, Ishaan Awasthi has trouble reading at school and viewed by the school, society, and family as lazy and punished constantly for his poor grades. His creativity and the talent for art are disregarded. The poor performance, misconduct, and unsatisfactory results of their child compel parents to send him to a boarding school where he meets an enthusiastic art teacher

Ram Kumar Nikumbh who effectively diagnoses the child's condition. The teacher comprehensively explains the condition of the child to his parents and helps the child overcome the disorder.

The movie is culturally significant in many ways though it seems an ordinary movie about dyslexia it explores the multiple shades of contemporary culture. First and foremost, it explains the ignorance and unwariness of family, society, and educational institutions about the reading and writing disorders of children. The high expectations of parents, society, schools that are not quite optimistic about students with developmental disabilities is effectively projected here. The society displayed in the movie is obsessed with success that demands effective performance and good scores marks in examinations. Throughout the movie, the message conveyed is that love, care, affection, and attention are essential in solving a child's dilemma and bringing them into the mainstream. Culture point of view ignorance, disposition for success, obsession, hatred, and negation are salient features of the contemporary society explored in the film.

My Brother Nikhil: A Revolutionary Attempt on screen (2005)

In recent years, Indian cinema has produced several experimental films touching on various sentimental issues such as gay and lesbian relationships, mental illnesses, AIDS, rape, molestation, dowry, oppression of women, and child labour.

The traditional cultural pattern of India does not allow a happy union of gay and lesbians. In society, the identity of gays and lesbians is recognized as lesser and hateful. The film *My Brother Nikhil* attempts to explore the dynamics of such relationships. The recent advancement of science and technology consolidated the point that gays and lesbians are the product of hormonal change and not the sin of previous birth. Gay and lesbians also have their own culture and identity. The film *My Brother Nikhil* showcases the subject of homosexuality from a universal standpoint. It attempts to raise a voice about the rights and identity of gays. It explores the aspect of the Goan lifestyle which became the accepted and preferred norms in modern India. Patients of HIV receive ill treatment in society. There are more rumours than facts in society about AIDS and its spread. The protagonist of the film contracts AIDS and finds support and solace in his boyfriend. The film made less benefit at the box office but made a serious attempt to explore the undisguised issues proficiently.

***Lagaan: Once Upon a Time in India*: The Projection of Urban Sensibility and Colonization (2001)**

This multi-starrer movie directed by Ashutosh Gowarikar with Aamir Khan explores in the lead explores colonial culture of British India. The setting of the film is a remote village in under the subjugation of revenue taxes implemented by Lord Cornwallis. It is a significant attempt to present Indian rural culture, the language of agriculture, administration, the enslavement of Indian people, and more importantly the rural ethos. The effective use of costumes and environment in the film opens up the realistic culture. The title of the film signifies the culture of revenue and wrong imposition on farmers. The approach of sophistication and manners of delegation of Britishers has been employed effectively in the film. The phase of the late nineteenth century and the dominance of the British Raj, as well as the suppression of Indians under various colonial rules is effectively depicted in the film. The words of Rosalind Hanton are very informative to comprehend the aesthetical significance of *Lagaan* as: "Beneath the tremendous variety in the empirical material of the subaltern studies historians: a long tradition of exploitation or a short-term economic dislocation, which provokes resistance and rebellion. Challenges to landlords or the agents of the state, the appropriation or destruction of the signs and instruments of their authority." (213)

From a cultural perspective, the film narrates the incidents of Victorian period and the rise of cricket in India. Today, cricket is a national religion of India and an inevitable part of Indian culture. The culture of globalisation and its wider spirit has efficiently elevated in the film. The cultural encounters between forward and backward classes successfully presenting the neo-imperialist concept of White minds over Eastern people is also reflected in the film. A movie with its setting in Champaran unfolds the extreme gender dominance and societal patterns of contemporary society. The reflected society in the film is male-dominated embedded with the caste system and traditional occupations. Agriculture is the only dependable source of income; many women and men are illiterate because they have to rely on translators or mediators to communicate with Mem Sahab. In brief, *Lagaan* explores the caste system, male dominance, and cross-cultural encounter effectively. The supremacy of White civilized culture and the inferiority of Indian culture are reflected in the expressions of white administrations but characters like Elizabeth signify equality and harmony who believe in love, justice, and humanity.

The present research article effectively explains the role of films in reflecting and exploring the Indian culture and cultural dimensions. Cinema being a medium of effective entertainment has successfully reached the sensibilities of the audience through experimental and creative film. Such films though small in number receive great appreciation and comprehensively perform the role of an effective weapon of social consciousness. The portrait of people they lives they lead is presented effectively. Moreover, the undisguised and unexplored voices of society found space in the films. Historical events, sensational subjects, a reflection of reality and representation have mirrored from multiple perceptions on screen. This establishes a significant place in films in the exploration and reflection of Indian sensibilities and culture.

Findings of the Study:

- The findings of the present study can be summarised in the following ways.
- Films are an effective and visible medium of cultural reflection.
- Experimental movies explore the dynamics of the subject in multiple perceptions.
- Realistic techniques used in films appeal to the senses of the audiences in films.
- The diversity of subject and liberation in film making brings liveliness in the expression of the message.
- Artistic films and experimental films play a pivotal role in enlightening the consciousness of people.

References:

Dwyer, Rachel. *Filming the Gods: Religion and Indian Cinema.* Routledge, 2006.

Gokulsing, K. M., and Wimal Dissanayake. *Routledge Handbook of Indian Cinemas*, Routledge, 2013.

Hanlon, Rosalind. "Recovering the Subject: Subaltern Studies and Histories of Resistance in Colonial South Asia." *Modern Asian Studies*, 1988.

Krebs, Katja. *Translation and Adaptation in Theatre and Film.* Routledge, 2013.

Laura Grindstaff, et al. *Handbook of Cultural Sociology*. Routledge, 2010.

Mehta, Rini B. "Colonial Indian Cinema." *Unruly Cinema*, 2020, pp. 19-60.

Needham, Anuradha D. *New Indian Cinema in Post-Independence India: The Cultural Work of Shyam Benegal's Films*. Routledge, 2013.

Rajadhyaksha, Ashish. "Indian Cinema." *Very Short Introductions*, 2016.

Culture: The Mirror of Society

Rohi Rani

Culture is a term that embraces every single activity of a being, it opens up all the hidden as well as unwrapped curtains of our society in which we live or exist. Culture exists within every human being. The main discrepancy between two beings isn't biological but cultural. It is having a bottomless hand on what we carry in our unconsciousness as Carl Jung said that our unconscious contains a multitude of archetypes in the form of myths, fairy tales, beliefs, etc. which are passed on to us from our ancestors. It is known to us that culture changes from society to society because it is man-made and is not inherited. In the light if these things, this chapter will present a picture of culture with reference to society.

Every society has its tradition, music, beliefs, laws, customs, habits, norms, mores, taboos, and ethics. It is the culture of the society which allows us to do few things that are acceptable publically and forbids few things that do not go well with the culture of our society. Culture isn't only connected with the material assets of our society but it has an equal impact on nonmaterial aspects as well. It is understood that a single thing viewed in a certain culture in someway can be viewed differently in a different culture. A particular thing, or item may have one fixed meaning in one culture but the same thing may have another meaning in another culture. Indian society is known for its diversity, here if a young boy or girl talks with an elder person while bowing down head and not maintaining eye contact indicates that a person is giving due reverence to his/her elder one whereas the same thing is viewed in a negative aspect in other country, this could indicate that you are not interested to talk with the person standing in front of you. So it is clear that a single behavior entails a different connotation. "Culture makes people comprehend each other to overcome barriers and promote harmony. It also develops the understanding to respect the political, social, cultural or regional variations. Paulo Coelho says 'Culture is not confined to a single attribute but is a merged whole. The ways and manners through which one eats are part of the culture, and it goes beyond a single attribute. Despite the striking differences in culture, we must remember that safeguarding our own culture does not mean contemplating others.

Edward Taylor defined culture as 'the multifaceted intact which consists our belief, morals, ethics, and other diverse abilities attained by a man'. Therefore, we can say that how and why we behave in a particular manner is the reflection of our culture and our culture leaves its traces from one generation to another and makes a ground for our society. Culture can be classified into two types.

1. Material Culture:

This type of culture is mainly associated with tangible things like buildings, vehicles, industries, etc. and the implication related to the success of an individual is taken on material assets because it mainly deals with the give and take process which mainly focuses on the comfort of our life so that our life would be trouble-free.

2. Non-Material Culture:

This type of culture deals with intangible things like our faith, belief, honesty, love, and commitment to ourselves as well as with people around us. Here, our world is based on trust, which is harder to build than material assets. It is hard to give and take someone's conviction. It has a big impact on the conviction of our life. This type of culture stresses the importance of human beings. It is based on the philosophy that if we have no tranquility, it is only because we have forgotten that we belong to each other. So, culture is not related to a single attribute but it is a complex whole that consists not only of what we have in terms of material assets but what sort of ideology we carry in our psyche which makes or creates our identity. The difference between two beings is mainly cultural which fills different colors depending on the culture we grow up in. This gives rise to acculturation, assimilation, and enculturation.

Acculturation:

It is the process of adaptation and acquiring traits from other cultures for equilibration in one's psychological space. It leads to amendments in our actions and beliefs. Acculturation only occurs in the charisma of another culture and people involved in this process have a particular intention behind it but they don't completely forget their own culture. They only adopt some traits from other cultures, for instance, a newly married girl learns the different ways and manners of dealing with different things at her-in-laws because it will help her to adapt to the culture of their family while still holding her own culture.

Assimilation:

It is the process in which a person completely isolates himself from his own culture and adheres to another culture for a long time. An example of assimilation is that a family from Kashmir migrates to America and after a few years their kids completely behave in a manner as Americans do. This includes language, dressing, eating style, etc.

Enculturation:

It is the process of learning one's own culture as we know that culture is learned not acquired. It is indispensable for an individual because every society needs civilized people which aren't possible without learning culture. The process begins after the birth of an individual and a child learns it in several ways, such as imitation, formal education, and informal education.

You must have seen that children while playing the different games imitate the different roles of their family members.

Culture has its impact on every aspect of our society, some prominent or dominant aspects are as:

Culture and Society:

Social scientists define, 'society as the group of people who share a common culture and develop a bond among different members of society which leads to the formation of different groups'. A renowned social scientist Emile Durkheim defines society as "a social product that is formed by the activities of different individuals through their deliberate attempts and thus forms mechanical and organic solidarity."

Mechanical Solidarity:

This type of solidarity is seen in primitive/ruler society in which the primary spotlight is given to *us* in comparison to *me*. Each part/individual cannot act independently. They must work together in a joint venture. For example, a clock cannot function if one of its parts isn't working properly.

Organic Solidarity:

This type of solidarity is seen in contemporary/urban society. It gives due importance to individuality in comparison to society. In organic solidarity, an individual has a similarity with a living body in which concord and consistency are produced by the interdependent operation of the parts. For example, a person can walk on one leg while losing one. Here a lot of emphasis is given to the division of labour which gives a push to individualism. Emile Durkheim called this by another name i.e. 'Egoism' and it becomes the core reason for several social evils. One among them is suicide which can be understood in four divisions given by Emile Durkheim.

1. Egoistic Suicide:

This stems from an individual feeling that no one is behind him and no one acknowledges a person the individual feels worthless and as a result, egoistic suicide occurs. There can be no denial of the fact that social acceptance matters a lot that is why Martin Cooley has said "I am not what I think I am, I am not what you think I am, I am what I think you think I am." This means consciously or unconsciously an individual gives much importance to social identity in comparison to personal identity.

2. Altruistic Suicide:

This happens because an individual becomes so much obsessed with others that a transaction starts to take place from self-love to self-annihilation. The individual sacrifices his/her life for the welfare of others.

3. Anomic Suicide:

This happens because an individual's resistance level drops and he isn't able to cope up with the given situation. This type of suicide usually stems from sudden or unexpected changes in one's life.

4. Fatalistic Suicide:

This is the last type of suicide as per Durkheim and occurs only because of the tight rules and regulations set by society. An individual is supposed to follow the line without questioning them. Long time exposure to this situation forces the individual to give up their life because they feel suffocated and choose death over life.

Culture and Women:

Although culture affects both genders equally, it has a greater impact on women. Say it their attitude or their penchant for culture, it dominates their every action. Cultural expectations draw a boundary between the different do's and don'ts for women. There should not be any gender specified roles in our society, we must change stereotypical perception or thinking that girls are meant for household chores like cooking, cleaning, fixing things, and others, these are the prerequisites of life and both genders should know how to cope with these things. In Indian society, women are labeled as being good or bad based on her tendency to 'please people' and men are believed to be straightforward for being good or bad. Differentiation is accomplished through canalization which involves the direction towards different things even in the preference of playthings. Girls are generally given soft toys and domestic appliances as the result, they mostly prefer indoor games like *Ghar-Ghar* in which they rehearse their adult expected roles such as mothers and housewives. While boys are given such toys that boost logical and aggressive behavior such as toyguns, bricks, balls, bats, and others. This double standard of society has become a reason for several evils. Chimamanda Ngozi Adichie_said, "Educate her that the concept of 'gender roles' is twaddle. Do not ever tell her that she should or should not do anything because she is a girl only because you are a girl is never the ground for anything ever". Nevertheless, we can't deny the fact that with time a lot has happened in favor of women, and now it is high time to change the cultural expectation so that a conducive society is formed. We have to live in alliance with each other so that a beautiful world will be formed where every wall will be painted with love, trust, honesty, loyalty, and peace.

Culture and Language:

Language is one of the best gifts human beings are endowed with. Language makes our life quite trouble-free because we can allocate what is revolving in our mind with the help of this. Ludwig Wittgenstein says, "Mastery over one language sets you in a corridor for life while mastery over two opens every door along the way." Language and culture are interwoven with each other in such a way that one cannot be identified without the other. It is very difficult to separate or understand them in the absence of one another. Language is seen as one of the important elements of communication. It is a process of interaction with others through which we share our ideas and beliefs but it is not as easy as it sounds. Most of the time, messages are transmitted through paralanguage i.e. (not what you utter, but the way you intimate your message). Human communication is complex and there is a danger of misinterpretation of things. So learning a language means learning the culture and customs of society, language is mostly the outcome of the thoughts and behavior of our culture and this behavior differs from society to society. India has 22 scheduled languages from Kashmir to Malyalam to Nepal. From this, we can safely conclude that how diverse cultural attributes are and the easy way to mingle with any culture is to know the diversity of language. Rita Mae Brown states that "language is the road plan of a culture. It enlightens you where its individuals came from and where they are departing."

Culture and Education:

As is the culture, so will be the aims of education. Culture lays the foundation for the educational system in any society. If a society gives more emphasis to spiritual themes of culture then the educational pattern will also stress on the same theme and pattern. The major reason for the variation of aims and objectives of education is cultural diversity. The main motive of education is to make its people civilized so that all individuals live a life of peace and harmony because education purposes polite and refined men rather than authentic men. John Dewey says that "Education isn't preparation for life; education is life itself." Education not only acculturates the individual but also plays a major role in the protection and diffusion of the same. Plants are produced by the process of nurturing and men by education. We are born scrawny, we need power; we need support; we need intelligence. We are not bestowed with everything at the time of birth but we can acquire everything with the help of education. Culture shapes society and controls the behavior of an individual by providing education. So we are liable to claim that culture and education are mutually complementary, supplementary, and interdependent in all micro and macro aspects that one can't function without the other.

Culture and Marriage:

Marriage is one of the social institutions of society which creates a union between man and woman socially and legally. It is known by different names such as wedding ceremony, *vivaha, nikah*, and others. Marriage is universal but the definition of marriage varies from one culture to another. It consists of many laws, rules, customs, beliefs, and attitudes that aren't universal. They are mostly dependent on the religion of a culture which influences the individual's opinion and expectation regarding the same. As we know India is well known for diversity so is the diversity in the customs and types of marriage from culture to culture. If we talk about the ancient times in India, there were different types of marriage like:

1. **Polygyny:** it is a type of marriage in which a man is allowed to marry multiple women at a given time. It was a usual practice in ancient civilization. At present, it is visible in some primitive tribes. It is further of two types:

- Sororal polygyny: In this type, the brides share the blood relation with other brides.
- Non-Sororal Polygyny: In this type, brides don't share any blood relation.

2. **Polyandry:** It is the marriage of one woman with several men at a given time. It is also of two types:

- Fraternal Polyandry: In this mode, several brothers share the same wife.
- Non-Fraternal Polyandry: In this mode, husbands don't share any relationship before marriage.

3. **Monogamy:** Here one man marries only one woman. According to Westermarack, monogamy is as old as humanity. It endorses affection for one another which is very difficult to find in the above-mentioned types. In this mode, woman enjoys her social status. This type of marriage is mostly visible in all cultures. It also has two types:

- Serial Monogamy: In most cultures, individuals are allowed to marry a second time due to divorce, death of a spouse, etc.
- Straight Monogamy: In this, the remarriage of the person is never permitted at any cost.

4. Group Marriage: In this mode, two or more women tie the knot with two or more men and children are regarded as the children of the entire group.

Rules of Marriage:

In Indian society, no absolute freedom is provided by any culture to marry as per the choice of the individual. Every society follows some rules. They can be categorized into two;

- Endogamy: In this, one has to choose one's life partner within a group. The marriage takes place within selected groups, castes, tribes, race, villages, etc.
- Exogamy: In this, a person has to marry outside his group. It strictly bans marrying within the group.

Apart from the rules, there are different customs and rituals performed by different cultures according to their religion. In Hinduism, the wedding (*vivaha*) is filled with several rituals varying from culture to culture. Whereas some rituals are seen in almost every culture such as *Kanyadaan* (father giving away his daughter to the groom) *Panigrahana* (groom holding the hand of his bride near the fire) and *Saptapadi* (taking the seven vows). Sikhs get married through a ceremony called *Anand Karaj,* here the couple walks around the holy book four times. Similarly among Muslims, the important ritual is *Nikah* along with *Mehar* (financial dower) to the bride by groom and signing the *nikah* paper.

To conclude, we can say that every society has different groups and every group has its own culture. Every culture is unique in itself. A civilized individual pays due respect to other cultures because the fundamental concern of every culture is the same and that is the exchange of love and respect.

References:

Haralambos and Holborn, *Sociology Themes and Perspectives.* 7th Edition. Collins, New York. 2004.

www.forbes.com/sites/forbescoachescouncil/2020/04/06/how-culture-impacts-our-value-of-women/?sh=216cce06474a

www.languagemagazine.com/blurring-the-line-between-language-and-culture/

www.mdis.edu.sg/blog/four-types -of-suicides/

Use of Culture and Tradition in *Kanthapura*: A Contextual Study of Indian Englishness

Dr. Amir Bashir

History has defined the intrigue of new fields and those fields which are interdisciplinary and nurtured the diverse sections of thinking, society, religion, politics, economy, culture, and art. This representation has itself come with certain speculations of newness to define the associations of society with its culture and has become a part of studies in several fields known as cultural studies. It's an academic field of interdisciplinary nature that took its roots from literary studies in the early 1960s in Britain. This is not a constraint; but is largely a part of cinema, television, advertising, print journalism, fashion, popular literature, and drama. It was a reaction against the alleged narrowness of literary studies who were concentrating only on the canon of high literary art. It is a recognized academic term used for the study of culture and cultures.

Cultural representations took place a high part in the literary dominance to evaluate the social stigma of its times, it evaluates cultural crisis and is co-related with the use of devices that authors use while writing and portraying the themes in their works. Similarly, this representation has been largely used by

Raja Rao in his famous work *Kanthapura* whose wide representation of myth and Indian culture in this novel make it a remarkable example for a different kind of language called Indian Cultural language, his use of myth and culture in the novel, is a story or in his language 'sthala-Purana or 'legendary history' associated with past and interference of present, the emergence of ignorance with awareness and some contemporary events. Raja Rao's *Kanthapura* discusses the problem of language while expressing thoughts and laying down the emotions and has entreated the English language with the local, regional words for the Indian Englishness. This article discusses the use of culture and tradition in the novel and emphasises the cultural interpretation of the Indian English Language.

Raja Rao was an influential writer of Indian fiction who initiated the use of actual cultural representations contributed to the growth and popularity of Indian English fiction and subsequently gave birth to the Indian Diaspora. The popularity of Indian English literature has gained the specific term 'Indo-Anglian-Literature' solely meant for the context of writing and works written by Indian authors or authors having Indian origin. If we look into the relative aspects of Indo-Anglian literature, some genres are classified under the category of post-colonial literature. The history of Indian English literature has witnessed the emergence of the Indian English language specifically mentioning the early works and writers, who used English unadulterated by Indian words to convey an experience and the sort of veneration to make the telling of their stories easy, in this context, Rao has rightly mentioned in his foreword to *Kanthapura*, "one has to convey in a language that is not one's own the spirit that's one own. One has to convey the various shades and omissions of a certain thought movement that looks maltreated in an alien language. I use the word 'alien', yet English is not an alien language to us. It is the language of our intellectual make-up __like Sanskrit or Persian was before but not of our emotional make-up. We are instinctively bilingual many of us write in our language and English cannot write like English. We should not. We cannot write only as Indians. We have grown to look at the large world as a part of us. Our method of expression, therefore, has to be as distinctive and colourful as the Irish or American." It serves a purpose of language of expression to the literary genres of Indian writers, especially the thought of writing an expression into English used by Rao is that of culture specifically used to imbibe the notion of social narrative in a different form and introduction of the use of myth, culture, and tradition, and its importance in the Indian society.

Myth and Culture:

According to the *Oxford Dictionary of Literary Terms*, "myth is a kind of story or rudimentary narrative sequence normally traditional and anonymous, through which a given culture ratifies its social custom or accounts for the origins of human and natural phenomena, usually in supernatural or bodily imaginative terms." In the contexts of literary domains, myths do have some historical basis and are distinguished from legends because of their less significance, but they have a similar mode of existence in oral transmission, re-telling, literary adaptation, and illusion. While as culture represents the established power to the resistance of identity of one's nation which infuses the taste of regional language to make it rooted with the origin of representation of their cultural life of the region and place from which the work belongs, and the roots of writer provides the authentication of writing at a cultural and social life. If we see the social representation of it, "myth came from the past whether it is true or not depends upon the roots of belief associated with the people, but due to some deliberate alterations or lack of evidence, it keeps changing". Although myths have been instilling influence on people and representation of it tells the story of an individual, sometimes it says about the supernatural events and any blind belief of people who follow carrying certain importance or belief whether social, religious, cultural, etc.

Recreation of myth and culture in *Kanthapura:*

Rao seems to be a high visionary, whose use of myths in the amalgamation of culture gave rise to the Indian English fiction with a taste of Indian Englishness. It was an attempt of recreating myths to display the cultural beliefs and quite a deliberate attempt to provide a new taste of emotions and feelings to his language. In the whole course of *Kanthapura,* Rao incorporates unique mythical techniques; incorporation of 'Harikathas' caste system, prejudices, display of Brahman, sudra, pariah, villagers, their life and movement of freedom in India have all reflected the taste of Indian Englishness while draining out the systematic order of writing in creamy English only. The emotional touch in his language provides a new establishment of some words and terms which was far from the understanding of a common modern Indian. He discusses many of its terms throughout the novel, making it a cultural language tool, while the narrations are only an attempt to make it Indian English. A fundamental principle of Rao's theory is the oneness of cultural obligation.

If we see the representation of the myths in the *Kanthapura*; it is an introduction of culture and narrative incorporation of presenting the culture on the plate which is a carryover of culture and myth together. Reflection of language is quite oblivios of his variation of words with Indian Englishness, he is the narrator, who begins with, "Our village-- I don't think you have ever heard about it—Kanthapura is its name, and it is the province of Kara". The reader happens to have the convention of emotionality, which had been deliberately adhered into its linguistic incorporation by the author to make it more cultural for the readers. Its narrator shares certain peculiar narrative techniques with the Puranas, It is a tale of a village told by a granny and a reflection of its oral heritage. The story is told in the form of Harikatha, and a mythical showcase of events in the story takes it to the very roots of the culture of the place of author. Gandhi's struggle for independence from the British, narration of Harikatha's in the only temple of the village, and the belief of people upon myth, Gods and Goddess. Raja Rao himself states that "it is impossible to separate reality from orthodox Advaita Vedanta". The author developed the cultural panorama of village and Indian tradition steadily. The locale in the novel is structured under certain regimes, where people follow religion and myth. This village is loaded with the fragrance of Indian sensibility, its unique identity of tradition, belief or religion, and much more which is akin to the cultural representation of the Indian social sphere. Raja Rao was quite a revolutionary, who with his use of mythical and ideal creativity had put an inspirational effect upon the Indian English literature of the 1930s. It was a literature of the Gandhian era which was inevitably influenced by these epoch-making developments in Indian life. When the Gandhian movement was at its peak, there was a nationalist upsurge which stirred the entire Indian society and its conscious awareness. Hence, with the novel, consciousness happens to be regimental part of writers to incorporate the suffering of Indian people, alienation of cultural depression, over which they were traumatized and called inferior, uncivil, unlettered and their linguistic inferiority for the English language remained as pain, even if they were authentic writers of English. It is out of this consciousness, Lionel Trilling defines fiction, "for our time the most effective agent of the moral imagination, emerges fiction" Hazlitt defines fiction as, "it is constituted of 'the very web' and texture of society as it really exists' and hence finds fertile soil in a society in ferment." This was not an attempt to make it a post-colonial presentation, but the established voice of that post-colonialism which occurred enduring the Gandhian era and the showcase of its impulse in the post-Gandhian era simultaneously came out with some compelling themes in which the ordeal of the freedom struggle, the East-West relationship, the communal problem, the plight of untouchables, the landless poor, the downtrodden, the economically exploited and the oppressed were predominant. Raja Rao has made the same formation of themes in *Kanthapura*, from its beginning to end seen in the narration, events, connectivity of thoughts, and social implication of the Indian society, caste system, and many more.

Myth, Culture, and Belief in the Novel:

The course of the novel starts with a cultural adoration in the context to make it more Indian with special relevance of religion, its social presentation of life and ethics, their belief and people. The protagonist is politically influenced who steadily creates a consciousness among the people of the village, whose sudden discovery of half-buried "Linga" which happens to be a central point for the political revolution. Moorthy appears to be a Brahmin, who digs out this "Linga" and creates a place for it which instantly becomes of importance and performing centre for all the festivals and religious rituals. Rao seems to be conscious of the cultural incorporations through the very display of his protagonist who amalgamates not only religion and culture but his role in making an influential political expression in the novel.

Moorthy is an influential figure with all the ideals of Gandhian spirit and ideology. His presentation in the novel is the representation of Gandhi, who was akin with the roots of his nation, Rao here deliberately inserted certain figure(S) of speech in the novel to vary the ideology of his character far from the culture of English. Moorthy discards foreign clothes, first of its impression of cultural disparity of his participation in the freedom struggle; he tries to save villagers, continues to be a freedom fighter and has been arrested. His sacrifices and struggle for the cause of his nation and villagers are all implied in the formation of their cultural importance. Implications of all such episodes had put forth the appreciation of understanding the text into the formation of culture and politics in the novel. Goddess Kanchemma is a protector for all villagers, while oneness in religion is portrayed, Rao hasn't kept away from the incorporation of the cultural fragrance of the village while giving us the description of the caste system. He chooses to discourse the carryover of all the ingredients of culture, social, myth, political and religious importance on its time. The variation in the generation of thoughts from shelf to shelf is serving the connectivity of Indian writers more appropriately with culture especially Rao who has not left even a single page of his novel without an impression of culture and myth in the novel *Kanthapura.*

Language and Indian Englishness:

The linguistic expression of the novel is Indian and the incense of cultural language has beautified the thoughts of the writer. Rao's subtle use of regional words is an observation of cultural compatibility with English. The holistic approach is evitable to English for taste. His use of words is formidably apparent to the culture of his village. Rao acknowledges thoughts with language. His representation of mythical incorporation of goddess Kenchemma the protector and described her in the expressions of these words:

O Kenchemma! Protect us always like this through famine and disease, death and despair. O most high and bounteous! We shall offer you our first rice and our first fruit, and we shall offer you sari and cloth for every birth and marriage, we shall wake thinking of you, sleep prostrating before you, Kenchamma, and through the harvest night shall we dance before you, the fire in the middle and the horns about us, we shall sing and sing and sing, clap our hands and sing:

Kenchamma Kenchamma
Goddess benign and bounteous
Mother of earth, the blood of life
Harvest-Queen, rain-crowned
Kenchamma, Kenchamma,
Goddess benign and bounteous

> And when the night is over, and the sun rises over the Bebbur Mound, people will come from the santur and kuppur will come from the santur coffee Estate… (*Kanthapura*)

Here, we have the attribution of myth and culture together to make the formation of thinking and sensibility which is a direct representation of Indian Englishness. Rao's use of English is indifferent to English itself, the expression comes in the formation of complex sentences to portray the culture and language. The variability of linguistic items and their use to paint the colour of Indian Englishness, such as, "We shall sing and sing and sing, clap our hands and sing." Rao and his use of diction culminates the tradition of cultural essence to a position from which the other expression of Indian English literature takes its place to be a variant for the use of other forms of literature in India.

Adding the use of emotional socialization in examining the events which demonstrate the attempt to show a critical view of race within the same community has brought forth the discourse of novel into the realm of context, as noted by Pramod K. Nayar in *Contemporary Literary and Cultural Theory*: 'Cultural Race Studies' (CRS) tries to emphasize race and ethnicity as key categories in the analysis of law, history, politics, and culture. Our concern here is with its cultural components, even, though and here we might mark its departure from poststructuralism

CRS cultural theories and studies are never very far from the social issues and themes in legal studies or politics."

If we see its basis, the rejuvenation of implying the cultural theories gave attention to the aboriginal literature and happens to be a nativist trend which shifts from the metropolitan written English to the oral, vernacular and regional. Literary culture is timely and politically significant. The same interpretation of signifying the events in the novel, which are politically and socially acclaimed with culture and regions akin with myths and beliefs within which they are resisting to keep an emergency of its footprints "was just a culture, belief and myth".

The demography of the Indian indigenous literature has happened to be post-colonial itself while carrying the representation of classicism and racism together. The political and social crisis have compelled the writers in general and Rao in particular to make an impression of the Indian English language. The entertainment of words rather than the translation of them had pasted the reality of emotions and culture in the language of the novel. The Indian linguistic identity has possibly segregated the actual English from the Indian Englishness while settling down the consequence of its terminology. The use of terminology in the text has chosen to be cultural and regional in its presentation to make it more akin to the soil of the author. *Kanthapura* is knitted with episodes from one end to another, in which the characterization and their importance have relevantly signified the very particular culture of life.

The ethnicity from culture and the display of the context are wide open to many discourses which accounts for the background analysis of themes in the novel. The sociable authentication of Rao has put many critics to call this text, a cultural study and a study of political scenarios. Although the deliberation of the protagonist creates a protocol of events through the discovery of Linga, and its gradual relation with the centrality of all the events in the novel. The development of culture and language speaks of the identity, and the transition of thoughts had brought the scene of post-colonial sense of speak. There has been a role-play of moral consciousness which ratifies the language of the novel. This novel brought many issues of cultural disparity into limelight and has discussed the various identical parts of cultural life with religion and especially the part of politics which frames the whole structure of people and their life, belief, and myths into a single image.

Using myth was a recurrent stance of Rao in the novel and simultaneously contributes to the culture at large. There has been an occurrence of myths regularly used in the past, an association that was quite avoidable to the bifurcation of English into Indian English, which mentioned tradition and belief of the culture and community into which they live. The discourse of culture attributes the meaning of texts which the author tries to convey in the text, with a conscious attempt to import the reality of any situation and to fulfill the conventions of the reader. The text of *Kanthapura* is the most influential while carrying these conventions into the assumptions of the text. The *Kanthapura* fulfills the readers' fantasies while making them imagine the time and events, sufferings of people, and cultural beliefs.

Kanthapura not only talks about the myths, culture, and politics, but it is an insight constituted of difference of culture, arbitrariness and ideology. The nature of cultural texts revolves around historical, anthropological, and ethnography which are stories about the situations, events, and people, marked by the usual structures of language and so with *Kanthapura* which is all akin to the basis of emotionality and roots of the culture of the author. New historicists opine that we must read the text as culture and look upon it as objects that can be 'read'. He carried objects while contemplating the marginal figures in the novels, like pariah Rachanna or anyone who is marginalized in the community with their subjectivities/identities/politics in the cultural formation.

In this context; new historicists like Greenblatt and Gallagher put it in a passage worth quoting for the adherence of *Kanthapura* as a text of culture. "There has been in effect a social rebellion in the study of culture, so that figures hitherto kept outside the proper circles of interest- a rabble of half-crazed religious visionaries, semiliterate political agitators, coarse-faced peasants in hobnailed boots, dandles whose writings have been discarded as ephemera, imperial bureaucrats, freed slaves, women novelists dismissed as impudent scribblers…"

The allocation of this description can be found in *Kanthpaura,* which carries all these themes in its womb to present a plate of objective studies of culture and tradition in the novel. From the representation of characters to events rather politics, religion, social and others creates a structure of that tradition and culture marked usually by the use of an unusual language. With impulse of the literary age of Raja Rao, many other factors became part of the stimulus for him to write about the culture and tradition.

The discourse of the *Kanthapura* takes the very forms of tradition and culture into the realms of keeping the legacy of Indian Englishness as important as English. The incorporation of linguistic items and the traditional use of morphological nuances imbibed the spirit of keeping the unity of language in the novel as culture. *Kanthapura* is essentially a text with all the ingredients of culture and tradition. The structure of narration and display of characters empowers the notions of culture and patterns of belief. The staunch appearances of the systematization of language with the unusual use of Indian/ regional words. The appearance of such words as; sahib, Gandhi Mahatma Ki Jai. Swamiji, mlecchas, pariah, etc, was cultural and traditional and far from the representation of the colonial English. In addition to its linguistic uniqueness, the novel's minute contextual appearance is not an attempt but rather just a way of expressing one's own culture and tradition.

Raja Rao textualized the history, culture, myth, politics, and has included the notions of everything in the novel by assuming the structure its very particular culture. The often use of being identical in the novel is what we define the culture and society from a very particular place with its relations. *Kanthapura* being social, cultural, political, mythical, and religious in the display of its contextual details becomes a tradition of what we call 'Indian' and Indian culture. There have been associations also with the power relations which were unequal and farther from the equal, and these cultural implications in the structures of power to enable a text for the creation of such ideas called culture and tradition. Hence, *Kanthapura* is the connection between culture and tradition that gives rise to authentic power relations in building up Indian society and belief. Rao was nationalistic in the identity of having his hands into something very colonial and modified the native versus foreign regime of writing and showcasing the events and tradition of culture and life.

References:

K. Nayar, Pramod. *Contemporary Literary and Cultural Theory*, Pearson. India. 2009.

Mukherjee, Upamanyu Pablo. P*ostcolonial-Environment: Nature Culture and the Contemporary Indian Novel in English*. Palgrave Macmillan, 2010.

K. Naik, M. *A History of Indian English Literature*. New Delhi, India. 1982.

Mulhern, Francis, editor. *Culture/Metaculture*. Routledge, London. 2000.

Akhada: Revolution of Women's Wrestling in India

Samrin Siddiqui

The present literary piece examines Post-Feminist discourses in the authorized book of the Indian wrestling coach Mahavir Singh Phogat's biography *Akhada* penned by sports journalist 'Saurabh Duggal'. His writing evokes a sense of authorship. This book marks the beginning of a feminist revolution in Haryana. In this book, Saurabh Duggal wrote about how Phogat's life took its way and prompted him to adopt the path of feminism and fight for women's liberty.

The book depicts Phogat's journey with his four daughters Geeta, Babita, Ritu, and Sangita hailing from small village Haryana to winning medals for the country. The story was popularized through the Hindi biographical movie *Dangal* in the year 2016 and suddenly brought the city Haryana into the limelight of respectability and whose story got greatly covered by the media across the world in the digital era. Mahavir's discourse deals with telling of his life events. It is a crucial step towards the changing discourse. Moments of his life are told and retold in magazines, television interviews, and film. His life explores the historical and cultural issues and Post-Feminist discourses that have impacted women's way of portraying.

Mahavir Singh Phogat's biography *Akhada* penned by sports journalist Saurabh Duggal evokes a sense of authorship. This book marks the beginning of a feminist revolution in wrestling in Haryana. The book depicts his journey with his four daughters hailing from small village of Haryana to winning medals for the country. Mahavir's discourse deals with telling of his life events. It is a crucial step towards the changing discourse. Moments of his life are told and retold in magazines, television interviews, and film. His life explores the historical and cultural issues and Post-Feminist Discourses that have impacted women's way of portraying.

Saurabh Duggal is a special correspondent with *Hindustan Times*, Chandigarh. His main area of interest is the Olympic disciplines. He covered the 2010 Commonwealth Games and 2012 London Olympics for the newspaper and was selected for the prestigious Inclusive Media–UNDP Fellowship 2015 to study sports as a vehicle for social upliftment, economic change, and women's empowerment in rural Haryana. The author describes the social and economic circumstances of the region. His writing depicts the lack of literacy and social life in the small village of Balali in Haryana, a state infamous for its practice of female foeticide and low literacy rates. Mahavir had to fight not just deep social stigma and an apathetic government, but also a disapproving family and personal tragedy to train girls in his sport. Due to Phogat's efforts, all his daughters have gone on to win medals and acclaim at the international and national levels, including at the Commonwealth Games and the Olympics. His story shares a message of courage and determination to prove his might and provide critical analysis of Post-Feminist identity.

Geeta Phogat won India's first-ever gold medal in wrestling at the Commonwealth games in 2010. Her sister Babita and cousin Vinesh Phogat are also commonwealth game 'gold medalists'. Her younger sister Sangita Phogat is also a wrestler. The main theme of the book is how sports as a vehicle can be used for social upliftment, economic change, and women's empowerment in rural Haryana. It discusses the notions of identity, uniformity, and the feminist revolution. It also discusses the condition of women after the feminist revolution and finds out women's struggle for survival in the face of domination, atrocities, oppression, and studies women's quest for identity.

Mahavir Singh Phogat challenged the social stigma and lack of literacy in Haryana. The study investigates how the protagonist empowers himself despite the various kinds of oppression and restrictions in his life. It is found that the causes of the protagonist's life problems and oppression can be classified into four categories: ignorance, patriarchy, stereotypical attitude, and sexism in Haryana. After reading a book, it is found that the women are deprived and denied basic rights and are dominated by patriarchy. The family struggles to break the shackles of patriarchy and achieve self-fulfillment and establish their identity.

Mahavir Singh Phogat uses five empowering strategies to empower himself comprised of making an assumption, experimenting, realizing, rejecting, resisting, and educating. By using these strategies, the Phogat sisters are eventually successful in freeing themselves from oppression and restriction. They finally are empowered and get real happiness. Women's status in Haryana has been a critical issue. Their lifestyle and how they are treated by society, state, family, and issues are highlighted in this study.

This biography focuses on Phogat's struggles in the modern world. He plays the role of a father, focusing on his real-life experiences which illustrate his fondest dreams, disappointments and specifically his lifelong resolutions against strong patriarchal beliefs that still exist in the present world. He uses his ideologies as a weapon to empower himself and is eventually successful in freeing himself from oppression and restrictions.

An honest attempt has been made to project Phogat's biography as one of the excellent examples of Post-Feminist discourses in the world of literature. In 2000, after the Olympic Games closed with much fanfare in Sydney (Australia), the legendary wrestler Mahavir Singh Phogat watched, heartbroken and dejected, as the prize reserved by his state government for winners of Olympic medals in wrestling was left unclaimed.

Determined to never see this instance repeated, Mahavir decides to do the unthinkable. Much to his neighbors' curiosity he spends two days digging a pit in his courtyard and asked his young daughters and nieces to join him in the task there at the break of dawn. Little did they know that this unusual command from him would change their lives. Yet, each of their wins in the ring, every ambition he had for them, came at great personal cost.

Women in Haryana have been shown constantly developing and changing. Women are portrayed mostly as round characters, which are initially bound and restrained by the chain of customs and tradition. His four daughters Geeta, Babita, Ritu, and Sangita are depicted as possessed by the demons of social taboos which are manmade and used to control the lives of the women. Their life depicts that women find themselves in the many horned dilemmas while going through such circumstances.

Mahavir Singh Phogat's biography is about the hope grit, passion, and determination of a young man in a remote area of Haryana who made his daughters compete with boys in wrestling. His passion for wrestling is overzealously depicted in the biography. It is the main text where his experiences are documented. His views and struggles are brought to light of the mainstream culture. His works and decision show true spirit and determination. A father played a crucial role in the development of culture as it has struggled against all forms of injustice. These four daughters and fathers also stand against the essentialism and sexism that was to pressurize to destroy them. His biography shares a message of courage, determination, and constant endeavor to prove their might and provide a critical analysis of postfeminist identity and repulsive dogma making him feminist.

The book highlights the gender prejudiced state of Haryana breaking all societal stereotypes. Saurabh Daggal's writing discusses the notions of identity, uniformity, the feminist revolution, and how a man trained his daughters to excel in male-dominated sports like wrestling. Mahavir Singh Phogat supported his daughters, decided to step in this display of courage. His cause is truly unique. His book reveals the issues of post-feminist ideology and identity in Haryana as well as in India.

It shares a message of courage and determination and constant endeavor to prove his might and provide critical analysis of post-feminist identity. This book shares a common goal: to define, establish, and achieve equal political, economic, personal, and social rights for women. This study analyses culture of Haryana. His biography is a model of a creative power that is found in his words that rebel against injustice. Phogat is helping to change the world. His passionate advocacy shows the power of aspirations for human rights to move history.

The work of Saurabh Dugal outlines his personal and artistic development, growth as well as his understanding of racial relations. He depicts his life along with his surroundings and historical changes at that time. His life defines feminism as equality for women and freedom from gender discrimination in different aspects of life.

The protagonist struggles for individual freedom, personal independence, equality, and the individual right to self-determination within the above theory exemplified and discussed. Furthermore, it also pointed out how womanish theology's claim relates to the beliefs, actions, and determinations of the protagonists in the book. The study reveals his daughter's life, facts, and miracles in Haryana. The study also clarified that there is ignorance, misconception, and inaccurate assumptions in Haryana.

Phogat's struggles not only against his culture, society but also from the patriarchal systems in a post-colonial scenario further complicate his ordeal and hinder his quests for liberty for his daughters. He explains how his life led him to embrace feminism and fight for women's rights. In the light of the discussion so far it can be concluded that Duggal's work has been studied and presents a woman of great courage and caliber. He is a feminist activist who challenged the power relationships and emerged victorious to a certain extent. For Phogat, the experiences, the history, the goals, and the ethics are patriarchal. This cultural story has been told from the perspective of a male. It provides no validation for his experience, no model for the articulation of his experience, no possibility to acknowledge his reality. The importance of writing for women is that without stories there is a sense in which a woman is not alive.

His work reflects aspects of the life of Haryana and the development of society over time. Several works are discussed that highlight various themes of post-feminist discourses, such as slavery, discrimination, and the quest for identity. His life is more complex and cannot be studied from a single perspective, it is a fact that he tries to focus on the problem of the quest for identity through his work. Therefore, an attempt is made to examine the quest for identity.

His daughters urge women to recognize and confront the present social context and identify themselves following their relationship to history. According to this biography, women should understand patriarchy and discover the oppressive nature of the patriarchal context. Women discover their whole unique selves, which are fulfilled mentally, physically, and spiritually. This biography reflects the various stages of challenges and means employed by them. In these discourses, Duggal has tried to surpass to overcome the first consideration of being a woman and to be at par with men. Phogat sisters succeeded to the extent that they successfully followed their chosen careers, asserted their rights to select their life partners, and professed their ideologies openly.

This chapter examines women's status not only in Haryana but also in India through the work *Akhada*, and how issues like nationality, religion, and feminist consciousness are portrayed in the biography. It also looks at how women as insiders reveal their subordination and submission through their lenses. This book *Akhada* contributes to the field of women's study in general and post-feminist Discourses in particular.

> *Always aim high, work hard, and care deeply about what you believe in. And, when you stumble, keep the faith. And, when you're knocked down, get right back up and never listen to anyone who says you can't or shouldn't go on.*
>
> —Hillary Rodham Clinton

References:

Adorno, Theodor. *The Culture Industry*. London: Routledge, 1991.

Aglietta, Michel. *A Theory of Capitalist Regulation*. London: Verso, 1979.

Naik, M. K. *A History of Indian English Literature*. New Delhi, India. 1982.

An Evaluation of Suicides in Indian Philosophy

Mr. Bonaventure Ikenna Jideofor

Traced to its etymology, "culture" is the English word of the Latin word "*cultura*" which means "to Cultivate". This meaning glows from the agricultural significance of culture. Hence culture 'cultivates' man and man inturn 'cultivates' culture. In the five-book compilations, the "*Tusculanae Disputationes*", the ancient Roman orator and thinker Cicero used the Latin concept "*cultura Animi*" to express the cultivation and growing of a philosophical soul. More so, culture has a deeper root from the Latin "*cultus*" which means "cult". It expresses the fact that culture exists as a form of cult. As a cult, some people belong to this cult and live by the values of such a cult. This makes evidence of the reality of cultural relativism. From this, Indian philosophy becomes a "cult" that expresses the values and thought-system of a people with a defined territory, with defined values and beliefs. Nonetheless, the philosophy of people exposes the culture, values, and beliefs of such people. In this way, man a product of his environment assimilates these values for his survival. Hence, an overview of Indian philosophy leads to the discovery of common characteristics embedded in the different systems of Indian philosophy. These common characteristics directly expose and emphasize the deep and objective values of Indian society. Through this, suicide, which has become a social, political, and religious concern, is placed argumentatively against the common values. Indian society is facing external and internal social pressure. It also presents the reoccurring facts of suicide as a seeming betrayal of Indian philosophy and values. In the end, through the excurses of cultural studies, the place of cultural materialism and its implications finds evidence.

Indian Philosophy: An Overview

While the scope of Indian philosophy is broad and elastic, it also has a resounding depth. In the *Journal of Indian Council of Philosophical Research,* Rajakishore Nath in his work: "*The Meaning of Life in Indian Philosophy: A Contemporary Reconstruction*" argues that all Indian philosophy is the philosophy of life. Unlike Western philosophy which is fundamentally a theoretical argumentation and intellectual analysis of the ultimate reality, Indian philosophy is a practical philosophy; a life philosophy. The religious, mythical, and ethical characters of the Indian philosophy make evident this claim. This position qualifies Indian philosophy as a philosophy laden with humanistic nature.

Nonetheless, as noted in *The System of Philosophy of Indian Philosophy* written by V.R. Gandhi, there are different systems of Indian philosophy: The *Sankhya*, the *Yoga*, the *Naya*, the *Mimamsa*, the *Vedanta*, the *Buddhism*, the *Hindu,* and the *Jainism*. It is to be noted that these systems vary in their perspectives yet, some characters are common in all of them. These characters become the concern of this chapter, through them the values of Indian philosophy are summarized and directed towards cultural studies on Indian soil with particular reference to suicide as a social vice. These common characters consistent with Indian philosophy include:

1. Philosophy as a practical necessity
2. Initial pessimism
3. Belief in an eternal moral order
4. Ignorance as the root cause of suffering
5. Liberation as the ultimate goal of life
6. Spiritualistic

Suicide as a Social Vice:

The word suicide is a combination of two Latin words; "*sui*" meaning 'of oneself' and '*cidium*' which means 'a killing'. Hence, suicide is the English word for the Latin

'*Suicidium*' which means 'the act of taking one's own life. It is the deliberate killing of one's self. Suicide, as a deliberate action one takes against his/herself to end his/her life directly, makes a sharp difference from euthanasia. R. G. Frey (1980) a contemporary philosopher and writer defines suicide as "a death which occurs intentionally as a result of a person knowingly, and willingly placing himself in perilous circumstances" (Shneidman 15). Frey critically underscores three major factors connected to suicide: one's will, knowledge, and intention. However, in the philosophical study of bioethics, suicide is categorized into direct suicide and indirect suicide. The first category underscores a conscious and direct action taken to immediately end one's life. The second category explains an action or non-action that leads to a slow death.

Though there are listed causes or reasons for suicide, yet Dr. Timothy J. Legg in the '*Encyclopaedia of Primary Prevention and Health Promotion* states that "there is no single reason that leads to the conclusion of someone taking his/her own life. It is often the accumulation of factors that increase the risk of suicide."(Pp. 11-12) While Dr. Legg argues that suicide is connected to mental disorders, he states that most people who commit suicide are mentally healthy before the act. Hence, he argues that depression takes the lead in the causes of suicide. In this way, suicide becomes the mismanagement of thoughts and ill reception of circumstances. Because of this, Victor Cosculluela, a psychologist in his work: "*Ethics of Suicide.*" asserts, "Every living organism has a life drive." For him, suicide happens when, "life-drive is overpowered by some other drive, i.e., taking risks, escaping from pain, etc." This directly marks suicide as a social vice; for if a man is driven by the principle of self-preservation and self-defence, to think and to act against such fundamental life principle is abnormal and a vice.

Suicide in India:

In the *Indian Journal of Psychiatry*, Lakshmi Vijaykumar in his work: "Suicide and Its Prevention: The Urgent Need in India" began thus: 'Suicide is an important issue in the Indian context. More than one *Lakh* (one hundred thousand) lives are lost every year to suicide in our country." He presents poisoning, hanging, and self-immolation as the common methods. Lakshmi lists the causes as follows: divorce, dowry, love affairs, cancellation or the inability to get married, and domestic violence. In further discovery, some factors are noted as more significant causes of suicide. They include the effect of modernization in India which cause change in socio-economic, socio-philosophical, and cultural areas of people's life leading to substantially high rates of suicide.

John Snowdon's work: "Indian suicide data: what do they mean?" recognizes suicide as a disease and notes that the rate of suicide in India is a concern. Thus: "addressing suicide in India is imperative to making a global difference in the burden of suicide" because India ranks among the countries with the high suicide rate. Given below list shows 2018 suicide data and their causes in India as stated by Statistical Research Department, Oct 16, 2020. Number of suicides across India during 2018, by cause:

- Family problems - 40,935
- Illness - 23,764
- Other causes - 16,849
- Cause not known - 14,828
- Marriage related issues - 8,284
- Drug abuse/alcoholic addiction - 7,193
- Love affairs - 5,342
- Bankruptcy or indebtedness - 4,970
- Unemployment - 2,741
- Failure in examination - 2,625
- Professional/career problem - 1,697
- Property dispute - 1,209
- Poverty - 1,202
- Death of dear person - 1,073

- Suspected/illicit relation* - 653
- Fall in social reputation - 524
- Impotency and infertility - 297
- Physical abuse (rape, etc) - 192
- Ideological causes/hero-worshipping - 94
- Illegitimate pregnancy - 44

As observed from a psychological autopsy study in India, the majority of people who deliberately kill themselves do not have a severe mental disorder. Hence it is stated: "Psychosocial stress and social isolation, rather than psychiatric morbidity, are risk factors for suicide in rural south India. From these facts; India becomes a concern for an evaluation of suicide. This is true because India is noted for its rich cultural heritage and philosophical depth. It then becomes worrisome in the context of cultural studies for a rich socio-philosophical society as India to have such suicides rates.

Evaluating the Common Characteristics of Indian Philosophy and Suicide:

As was discussed, the scope of Indian philosophy is broad and deep. In this case, the common characteristics discovered in Indian philosophy are to be the compass on which an evaluation is to be established.

1. Philosophy as a Practical Necessity:

Indian philosophy is qualified with a humanistic nature. In Indian thought, philosophy seeks to solve existence struggles and to make life livable. It is therefore not a mere speculative activity by a mode of living. Hence philosophy in India and life are inseparable. This makes Indian philosophy a practical necessity; to live happily and maintain serenity, philosophy must be applied. Thus, Sacar R. Murgai in his work *Indian Culture* states that, Hindu is a philosophy of life. For Hindu philosophy "if one lives a pious life in the service of humanity and does not think evil, do evil and see evil, *Moksha* is attainable" that is, freedom from the cycle of birth and death is attainable. From this background, suicide presents itself as taboo since in Indian philosophy "life is the same in everyone and every form of life should be respected. By this, to take one's life is to disrespect life, it is also to think evil, do evil as it causes harm to the family of the dead.

In its peculiarity, The *Aryans* believe that human life is divided into 4 stages:

1st Stage: Brahmacharya up to 25 years: one is expected to acquire education.

2nd stage: Grahasta Ashram From 25 to 50 years: one is expected to lead a family life.

3rd Stage: Vanprasat Ashrama 50- 75: one is expected to get rid of the responding and devote time to meditation and reading of philosophy.

4th stage: Sanyas 75-100: leave the world. Live in the Jungles and devote your life to learning, prayer, and worship of God.

It is to be noted that Lakshmi mentions that "the majority of suicides in India are those below the age of 30 years: the fact that 71% of suicides in India are by persons below the age of 44 years imposes a huge social, emotional, and economic burden on our under spiritual". Concerning the Aryans, suicide should be absolutely out of the picture because as a practical necessity it does not fall into any Horizon. Hence, if these divisions of life are followed, one will be too busy to actualize suicide. The universal truth of Buddha, the four noble truths, and the Eightfold path. All of these directly strangle the possibility of suicide in Indian society. Thus, the awareness of suffering, awareness of Right effort, Right Mindfulness, Right Concentration should quench the actualization of suicide since *nirvana* assures the end of suffering when the eightfold path is followed.

From these, the increase of suicide in India raises suspicion on the neglect of her philosophical wealth.

2. Initial Pessimism:

Indian philosophy expresses a doctrine that reality is essentially evil. Emphatically, as in other systems, the Sankhya system of philosophy argues that there are 3 kinds of misery in the world.

1. Misery due to oneself (*Adhyatmic)*

2. Misery due to the products of element (*Adhibhotic)*

3. Misery due to supernatural (*Adhidaevic)*. For them, the total cessation of these miseries is the absolute end and objective of man.

This dissatisfaction led to the development of new thought systems and philosophies that would save humanity and elevate man above the misery and pain he suffers. Hence, Indian philosophy argues that man can maneuver suffering and attain liberation (*Moksha*). It is therefore, illogical that suicide yet exists to a worrisome degree in India. The awareness of this supposed pre-existing suffering and misery in the world should logically necessitate a happy and optimistic worldview in Indian society. The awareness of initial pessimism should in its unique way treat the psychology of Indians to abhor the actuality of suicide in society.

3. Ignorance as the Root Cause of Suffering and Liberation as the Ultimate Goal:

Human suffering understood in Indian philosophy is fundamentally caused by ignorance; man suffers because he does not know. As found in Indian philosophy, ignorance leads to the attachment of worldly values or objects; a form of materialism. This attachment enslaves man and hinders him from acquiring the right knowledge of ultimate reality. Hence freedom could be achieved by using the right knowledge. Knowledge in this context then becomes a fundamental tool for freedom and joy. Hence, it is through the acquisition of the right knowledge of things that man escapes suffering and attains freedom. This common feature of Indian philosophy does not allow the possibility of suicide when understood and applied.

Furthermore, liberation as the ultimate goal of life as found in Indian philosophy points to the fact that man is troubled in the world. As defined in the Indian context, "liberation means complete cessation of suffering' (kkhsou). It is commonly agreed in Indian philosophy that liberation signifies the end of the miseries of life. Hence, there are Four ends (*purusartha*) of human life that are notable in Indian: philosophy: *Dharma* (merit), *Artha* (money), *Karma* (desire), and *Moksha* (liberation). Among these, *Moksha* is considered the ultimate goal of human life, (kkhsou). More so, there are three paths for the attainment of liberation: Knowledge (*Jnana*), devotion (*bhakti*), and action (*karma).* A critical and objective analysis of these paths immediately underscores how much the paths towards liberation can fortify one against environmental pressure which leads to depression and suicide. Hence, through "knowledge" one becomes aware and conscious of his environment and the pressure it creates; the act of devotion leads to calmness and serenity of mind and body; through right action, one attains fulfillment and productivity. Hence suicide is not entertained.

4. Belief in an External Moral Order and a Spiritualistic nature:

In Indian philosophy, except for the *Carvaka* holds a materialistic system; Indian philosophy acknowledges a belief in the extended moral order. This order has different names as varies by each thought system but they all express a fact that no one should violate or offend such moral order since each action has its consequences. Furthermore, Dr. S. Radhakrishnan an Indian philosopher and Statesman asserts that Indian philosophy is essentially spiritual. This is true because the spirit or soul in Indian culture is believed to be superior to the body. Form this, Indian philosophy has spiritual values attached to it. This spiritual character aims at living a disciplined moral life emphasizing the superiority of "spirit" over "matter".(KKhou).

The acknowledgment of an external moral order in Indian society and the spiritualistic nature of Indian philosophy should nurture resilience and fortify the emotional structure of the people who abide by the culture of Indian society. By this, the actualization of suicide is immediately met with oppression and rejection. The uncertainties of life judged from the Indian socio-philosophical values should not lead to deliberate killing of oneself because the awareness of the spirit over matter should develop a sense of pressure management, psychological pain relief, and escape of materialistic concern.

From the above stated, Indian philosophy is observed to be closely knit with ethics, religion, and psychology. In this regard, Gandhi in his work *The Systems of Philosophy* asserts:

> Every religion has its philosophical as well as ethical aspect and the latter without the former has in India at least no meaning. If every religion has its physical and ethical side, it has its psychological side as well. There is no possibility of establishing a relation between physics and ethics but through psychology. Psychology enlarges the conclusions of physics and confirms the idea of morality.

Cultural materialism in connection with the high suicide rate in India:

Cultural materialism among all other contemporary concepts is a concept that came to life from the intricacies that surround cultural studies prompted by Hoggart's *Use of Literacy* (1957) and Raymond Williams *Culture and Society* (1958). As a field of study, Nasruallah Mambrol defined Cultural Studies as "an academic discipline which combines political economy, communication, sociology, social theory, literary theory, media theory, film studies, cultural anthropology, philosophy, art history/ criticism, etc. to study cultural phenomena in various societies". Further, he asserts that "cultural Studies researches often focus on how a particular phenomenon relates matters of ideology, nationality, ethnicity, social class, and gender."

Based on these definitions and their implication in the context of cultural studies, suicide becomes a phenomenon that matters around the world. This signals repulsion of certain cultural practices, and seeming neglect of Indian philosophy as a way of life. In other words, it is a manifestation of cultural materialism.

Cultural materialism is a combination of two concepts. The qualification of culture with Materialism is a borrowed idea from Karl Marx and Friedrich Engel's dialectical materialism and historical materialism. As it is, "materialism" is the belief that history is changed and progressed by material factors rather than ideas that make 'matter' superior to 'idea'. For Karl Marx, society faces evolution through material forces which causes a shift from its status quo. This change occurs through a process called "class struggle" or "class conflict". However, it would be misleading to imply Karl Marx's idea on dialectical materialism against the concept of "cultural materialism."

Cultural materialism first saw light through Marvin Harris's book *The Rise of Anthropological Theory*. Cultural materialism in Harris's thought has an anthropological orientation. However, the theory of cultural materialism argues that there are three distinct levels of social systems that explain the cultural change: infrastructure, structure, and superstructure.

Infrastructure describes how basic needs are met and how they interact with the local environment. It consists of "material realities': mode of production (technology), mode of reproduction (population), and social practices by which society fits its environment. On the other hand, the structure consists of the economic, social, and political organization of the society. And the superstructure is comprised of ideology and the symbolic representation of society. Harris argues that infrastructure is the force that influences other levels that is, structure and superstructure. From this, since the causes of suicide in India rank highest around social issues in the likes of family problems, divorce, unemployment, marriage-related cases, failure in examination and more and that young people take the lead in taking to suicide in India, it therefore, creates a suspicion of external pressure in Indian society which could slowly linger through Harris' three levels of the social system.

Furthermore, in 2018 and 2019 family problems were the leading cause of suicide in India as recorded by Statistical Research Department and The National Crimes Record Bureau respectively; "according to report, among people age above 18 and below 45, family problems were the biggest report cause of suicide." thus, the repeated statistics on the family problem as the leading case of suicide in Indian points to the tendency of "suicide contagion" as defined by The U.S. Department of Health and Human Services) in Indian society, because Indian family structure makes this case viable. Hence, a common problem finds a common 'solution' since suicide and suicidal attempts have earned relevance in the media. WHO understands suicide as a vice to have given guidelines on suicide reports. Lakshmi in "Media Matters in suicide- Indian guidelines on suicide report" discloses these guidelines thus: that newspapers and news agencies must NOT:

- Place stories about suicide prominently and unduly repeat such stories.

- Use language which sensationalizes or normalizes suicide or presents it as a constructive solution to problems
- Explicitly describe the method used
- Provide details about the site/location
- Use sensational headlines
- Use photographs, video footage, or social media links.

These guidelines relate to the minimization of suicide contagion. Therefore, the Indian cases of suicide ranking high around young people and family problems poke the existing infrastructure in India. However, beyond cultural materialism, the reoccurring data of suicide in India raises suspicion on the neglect of her philosophical wealth; a negation of Indian philosophy as a practical philosophy.

While it is complex to determine the level at which suicide could be entirely called a mental disorder, R. G. Frey's definition of suicide as a result of a person's conscious effort to place oneself in perilous circumstances makes it entirely difficult to leave suicide on a mental disorder pedestal; knowing and willing are intentional actions. Therefore, it anchors suicide based on determined action. From this, Indian philosophy in its essence triumphs over the actualization of suicide when held as a practical necessity. But social pressures have their way of undermining an established principle.

References:

Gandhi, V.R. *The System of Philosophy of Indian Philosophy,* Shri Mahavira Jaina Vidyalaya, Bombay, 1970.

Legg, Timothy J. *Encyclopedia of Primary Prevention and Health Promotion.* New York: Author Press, 1999.

Covid-19 Narrative: A New Normalcy

Khushnudha Mehraj

Human beings are integral part of society. They support life on earth but it is declining as the Covid-19 pandemic has caused a health crisis in recent times. It has been a sudden disruptive event that has affected populations across the globe. There have been 25 million confirmed cases of Covid-19, the scale of death toll reached to a figure of 850,000 and 17 million people have recovered also. The pandemic brought the risk to human existence and halted human activities. In addition, scientific technology solutions were of no use. This intensified fear and anxiety among people. The Covid-19 pandemic changed the way how the global population believed, lived, and acted. The pandemic ruptured and disrupted the normality among people. It led to deep suffering and loss, and at the same time affecting the lives of people abruptly. The major interruption to the global economy, lack of funds had the worst impact on the worldwide situation. On the other hand, some changes were viewed positively for the environment, rapid decrease in pollutants and decrease in noise pollution. The human relationship with the environment is no longer sustained as we have affected our environment, destroyed the habitats and resources on a global scale by overexploitation. Over a small period, we have witnessed global changes due to pandemics. The Covid-19 has given us a chance to reconsider our relationship with nature and a need to remind our dependence on this world. It made us realize that how humanity is dependent on its well-being. Despite notable perturbation of Covid-19, this had led to a heightened impact on society. The efforts like social distancing meant to promote the well-being of people resulted in the isolation of people. The impact of Covid-19 resulted in deteriorating mental health across the globe. During the last past decades, there has been an increase in the rate of suicides due to mental breakdowns. But it is important to emphasize that loneliness has now become an intensified phenomenon generated by coronavirus or we can say by the necessary social distancing.

Uncertainty was correlated with anxiety, apprehension, and trouble, according to the research. The considerable changes that we faced with new realities affected our lives like work from home, online-schooling of children, unemployment, and lack of physical contact with the family and close ones. The survey from March 2020 around the globe provides data on the devastating impact of Covid-19 on mental health. Countries reported far-flung disruption on mental health issues. The different factors which are responsible for the distress on isolation related to the lockdown measures were psychological, sociological, cultural, environmental aspects of Covid-19 which leads to driving the loneliness caused by the pandemic.

Social Aspect:

With allusion to the current pandemic crisis, we have come across the fear and anxiety of losing our close ones, of being alone, of infecting someone or getting infected. Persons with the possibility of contact with the infected were asked to stay in isolation to reduce the risk of getting infected. Social distancing was taken as a global measure but it induced frustration and boredom among people. Human communication and support were lost. It led to traumatic stress. It was an alienation from the community itself. Social distance has affected the relations among people and their perception of sympathy towards others. Separation from closed ones, helplessness, isolation, loss of freedom leads to anxiety among people. Symptoms such as suicidal tendencies and emotional enfeeblement became worse.

Ostracism in Covid-19:

The pandemic brought severe changes to people's lives. People start living differently than before Covid-19. For example, people usually used to go out for a family get-together and spend time with their relatives and loved ones before the pandemic. The prevention of coronavirus lead to distressing family quarrels and affected family relationships. Heartbreaking stories and sufferings of families have been experienced. Moreover, as a result of Covid-19, the emotions, care, and support towards family relations were lost. Disturbing stories abound of individuals who were suspected of covid-19 were treated as a curse to society. For example, if a person would recover or be discharged to his home after a long time, the person would not get any emotional support from the family. Even other relatives would suddenly refuse to show alternating care and the residents in the neighborhood would be afraid to make any contact with them. The houses of the patients were treated as haunted houses. The irony is that Covid-19 has exposed the harsh realities of people, tall claims of relatives that they are there for us were shattered when relatives instead of giving support to each other remained apart in desperate times. We have seen many funerals attended only by health workers instead of family members. This social ostracism resulted in psychological problems in people who suffered from Covid-19. They felt like sinners and faced greater levels of anxiety and depression.

Marital Conflict:

The environment created by the Covid-19 had put high pressure on society that led to a rise in marital conflict. There has been an increase in divorce cases, struggling marriages during covid times than its preceding years. These conflicts started uprising from lockdown. As we have seen in many countries, couples anticipate divorces. Confinement led to pessimistic relationships and harmful interactions between partners. Being separate gives them an escape from the clash; however, Covid-19 had put them in convenience which leads them to aggression. The reasons might be the housework, differences of opinion, childcare, unemployment and so on.

Domestic Violence:

Globally, domestic violence has risen due to the Covid-19 lockdown. Regardless of the chaotic scenario created by the Covid-19 individuals have found themselves in confinement. The reports have shown that domestic violence had shown a rapid growth right after the catastrophic event. In a lockdown, workplaces were shut and people spending time together with their families resulted in quarrels. This is the result of the psychiatric consequences of pandemics. In this scenario increased spousal abuse has been reported which has been the major reason for self-harm or suicidal thoughts. Therefore, increased incidences of domestic violence have a considerable impact on mental health. There have been numerous cases of women who have faced trauma and revealed their anxiety levels due to a stressful environment and unfavorable financial conditions at home.

Cultural Aspects:

Across the globe, multiple factors affect culture. The interruption caused by Covid-19 led to a fall in the economy in terms of international trade, finance, investment, construction, and global production. The overall global economy has reduced significantly. Trade restrictions and restraining measures prevented farmers from buying and selling their production, workers from reaping crops and thus disrupted the economy. There was a sudden decline in demand for goods which led to a collapse in the economy.

Cultural Transaction:

Covid-19 pandemic had enormous consequences on the relations of different countries. A global crisis has resulted from Covid-19 from a community to a nation. It has triggered multiple descending in every aspect of our lives. It involved systematic disruption and uncertainty collectively. China and Wuhan experienced severe crises during the first stage of Covid-19, they became involved in cultural traumas. They were blamed for spreading coronavirus which leads them to struggle across the globe. It evokes a sense of loss and anger as a result all countries experienced serious damage in trade and national economies. Also, it intensified the enmity between the countries USA, India, and China. The blame game was played all over the world over the cause of the pandemic. The relation between China and India was already in shambles after the Galwan attack by China in which India lost 20 soldiers. In Covid-19 the relationship got more complicated, trade tensions got exacerbated which affected the economic relations between them. However, Chinese products were boycotted not only in India but outside as well. The irony is that India is one of the biggest importers of Chinese goods. Several media channels have called for boycotting Chinese products however, the advertisement they display belongs to Chinese smartphones. A recent report of Global Times warned boycotting goods from China would be dangerous and led to India's economic degradation. Therefore Covid-19 segregated the boundaries between the countries.

Racist Attacks:

The pandemic has released a disaster of hate and xenophobia which resulted in racist attacks in society. There have been several reports of racist attacks across the globe, the Covid-19 crisis led people to demonize foreigners, Chinese or Asian people. The Asians have been targeted with derogatory language in media, statements by politicians as we have seen in one media incident of Donald Trump where he disgraced a Chinese journalist from BBC with his disparaging remarks. Also, U.S President Donald Trump's use of the "Chinese virus" has promoted the use of hate speech. Around 1500 incidents of racism were reported. Many politicians of other countries also put forward their discriminatory statements which led Asian people to suffer across the globe. They were subjected to racial attacks, beatings, bullying, threats, and abuses that appear during a pandemic. In India, Muslims were being targeted for spreading the virus deliberately.

Plague and Caste:

According to the studies, in India, the population of Dalits, Muslims, and women is lesser in comparison to other citizens in other groups. Even though when the whole world was going through the phase of Covid-19, it didn't change theoutlook of the Upper classes. The minorities still face discrimination; they were given poor health care facilities that were not enough to combat the disease. Other examples were the Dalits, how they were trapped and marooned in different cities with no source of support. Most of them are labors who suffered from no access to food, water, and essentials. Thousands of labours from different states went back to their villages by walking hundreds of kilometers. Many of them died on roads, never reaching to their villages. Covid-19 suspects were treated as untouchables. They were stigmatized, and untouchability became common. Nobody would enter the house of Covid-19 patients even though if they had recovered.

Psychological Aspect:

On a psychological level, it is about the subjective experience of individuals. The main characteristics to be considered here would be age and job status. Economic decrease and delays in academic career affected day to day life. It induced a higher level of anxiety among people. The pandemic has eradicated jobs and placed millions of lives at risk. Employees suffered due to uncertainty concerning their job or future which led to stress and agony. The economic disruption caused by the pandemic proved devastating. Estimated millions of people are at risk of falling into poverty. Across the globe, workers were unable to feed themselves and their families during the lockdown. These testing times indeed led to suffering particularly small-scale workers. Transportation being hardest hit faced high levels of poverty due to lack of income. The feelings of hopelessness and desperation among people led to panic attacks or hysteria. This gave birth to severe psychiatric conditions which resulted in negative outcomes like suicides and elevated anxiety.

Impact of Quarantine:

Travel and communication are possible for every individual across the globe, but during the Covid-19 phase, travelers were restricted and forced to live in isolation. This led to feelings of disappointment and vexation. People were unprepared for the drastic change in their lives, which rendered them helpless and frail. Separation from loved ones, boredom, and loss of freedom lead to post-traumatic stress symptoms, madness, and chaos. Quarantined staff was more likely to report insomnia, poor concentration, and deteriorating work performance. There is much evidence that has shown the significant impact of mental illness on health workers as well. Being unable to go to their respective homes, health care worker status was also related to psychological effects. The results suggested that there are many consequences that affected them not just the people who are in quarantine but also the health care system.

Impact on Old Age groups:

Of all age groups, adults above the age of 60 were reported to have severe complications, requiring hospitalization, needing intensive care unit treatment including a ventilator. This led to intense fear and anxiety among adults. Unfortunately, it led to the avoidance of old people by impelling them to sit in isolation. This had led to a direct impact on their mental health by the lack of social contact. The horrendous effects of Covid-19, unfortunately, impacted older adults. Many of them did not have access to the internet, social media platforms that can deviate their minds to prevent anxiety. These social platforms are nowadays used by younger generations as they remain socially active for human interactions. There is also a fact that many old age people are already isolated by living separate, widowhood, and so on. In old age, people face challenges every day to survive. Attention should be paid to the consideration of old people or we can say the pandemic might be a life teaching lesson to know the importance of old people to society.

Pursuance of Life:

The pandemic had transformed people's way of perception. People start searching for meaning in life. This led them to pause from performing their specific roles in life and forced them to look into their souls. They start finding the meaning of life, what matters in their lives. They have begun realizing the meaningless value in wealth and fame. They have become anxious and tense after facing reality which affected them psychologically and stressed them.

Survey of Mental disruption:

A survey by the WHO from March 2020 found that 89% of countries are experiencing mental and neurological trauma caused by the Covid-19 virus. It emphasizes the acute need for mental health investments. Isolation, unemployment, fear, and poignancy were activating mental health conditions. People across the globe faced increased consumption of alcohol and drug use like in the case of India, we have seen when the lockdown was eased, people came out on roads without maintaining social distance. The mental dilemma pushed people into risky situations as they had lost control of their mindsets. Many reports came from across the globe that people were dying by suicide after they failed to get liquor during the lockdown. As people were frustrated and experiencing a mental breakdown. The alcohol that used to cost Rs 500-600 was being sold for Rs 1200-2000, black marketing of liquor was on the grounds. In the U.S sales of wine increased by 50% compared to the previous year 2019. The online sale of liquor resulted in a massive increase in alcohol production. The same practice was followed by other foreign countries like in the U.K, where sales of alcohol jumped abruptly. Other reports have found an increase in tobacco from 12% to 25% for smoking. The intake of smoking cigarettes has now become an addiction. This has shown the impact of Covid-19 which has caused mental disruption. On the other hand, reports surge about opioid use in the wake of unemployment and isolation. The survey conducted by the Centers for Disease Control and Prevention (CDC) shows the psychological and emotional impact of Covid-19 across the globe. It found an increase in the percentage of drug abuse than the previous year 2019. The hardships faced by the people lead to the addiction of drugs currently the common example is unemployment. The jobless people are highly on opioid consumption. They are currently seeking medical help, therapies to restrain drug use.

The outbreak of Covid-19 drastically affected the entire world that people had never imagined. It became the reason for so many impacts on humanity. Millions of people encounter an existential threat. The countries with humanitarian crises or emergencies are subjected to the effects of Covid-19. It led to uncertainty or we can say these were the crucial times in addressing the human dimensions. A deep understanding of the context of the current situation and the role of aspects in the impact of the Covid-19 pandemic shows us the indivisibility of all rights of humans. It has made us realize the importance of appreciating things around us. Unfortunately, it has taught us the reality of the world, how humanity is more than the Covid-19. It has disrupted and affected every aspect of life whether social, cultural or psychological. They all affect in one way or another, our well-being. As coronavirus has exposed class-based vulnerabilities, toxic inequalities, and lack of humanitarianism, this is because of incurable egoism among people and those who proclaim themselves as idols of morals regardless of lack of humanity. The coronavirus did not attack the particular person, it attacked the society collectively from every aspect. Ideally, it should unite us for the well of mankind and can help us to overcome the overall recession. All we can do is rethink before acting for our future and tackle our challenges with ambition and moral values. Our purpose should protect and promote human dignity and the welfare of society. Also, we must maintain the world's stability to cope with the upcoming challenges. It's time to break all stereotypes and finally start acting on a righteous perspective. Only then we can make this world a better place to live and ascertain that our 'new normal society' should be a better one.

References:

Centers for Disease Control and Prevention, Health Equity Considerations and Racial and Ethnic Minority Groups. 2020.

Coronavirus in the U.S.: Latest map and case count," New York Times. 2020.

D. Puras. "Covid-19 and mental health: Challenges ahead demand changes," *Health and Human Rights Journal*. Vol.1 Issue 2 (2020).

The Poignant Depiction of Subaltern Women in Mahasweta Devi's *After Kurukshetra*

K. Dhureshavar

This literary article attempts to explore the idea of Agency as seen in Subaltern Women and how they have resisted regaining their individuality within the context of a gendered society. Who are the Subalterns in the context of the three collected stories by Mahasweta Devi is a complex question to answer. Spivak in her essay, 'Can the Subaltern speak? says that, 'a subaltern is someone who does not have any access to the ideological root of power.' Often the word 'subaltern' is equivocated in a singular sense directing its meaning to a group or an individual who is oppressed by a superior power. The hegemonic structure is considered to be orthodox and people who have limited access to such powers are treated as subalterns. This idea strategically gives preference to patriarchy in a constructed social organization. The basic question of human rights is attacked by the so-called subalterns and technically it becomes gendered. Though there might be a world of difference between a male and a female, it is inappropriate to position them based on superiority/inferiority because it tends to disrupt the idea of humanity in general.

In the first two stories, *The Five Women* and *Kunti and The Nishadin*, there are many hierarchical positioning between the women themselves who belong to the rajavritta and the lokavritta. Mahasweta Devi by giving voice to those who were left unheard in the Grand Epic is subverting the position of rajavritta women in this text. The significant outcome of such a shift in perspective has resulted in an agency of change within the subalterns. Be it the five women, the Nishadins, or Souvali, they are comfortable within their own home (Kurunjangal, Forest, and 'the margins of the town' (of Hastinapur)). The lokavritta women do not see their home as a marginalized space.

Devi, by using sentences like "They were walking back to the outskirts of the capital city." (Devi 2) "On the margins of the town live the marginalized" (Devi 45) has stressed and pointed out the position of subalterns by marking out their territory. By doing so she calls attention to the fact that they don't have access to the collective national identity of the local government. The five women are not comfortable within the space of rajavrittas because their way of living and practices are culturally and sociologically different. Kunti's position in the second story is reversed because she is brought to the location of the lokavrittas. Kunti neither understands nature nor the people (Nishads) who dwell in the forest. In *Souvali*, Mahasweta Devi has shown a history of violence that had been silenced which is far removed from the past and the time of the Kurukshetra War. We can see Dhritarashtra and Gandhari as a couple who has dehumanized the existence of Souvali and Souvalya. The struggle to recover their lost humanity is achieved when Souvalya had done the last rites of Dhritarashtra though he was never recognized as his son, a Kaurava.

The choice of partial displacement through an agency of power can be seen in the first story *The Five Women*. Madraja, the head dasi, is an agent of power. Her position gives her the license to control both sides. She has control over the rajavritta queens and the lokavritta women. She recruits members of her clan from Kurunjangal to help the pregnant Uttara. Agents are simply the products of their culture; they work with a goal. Madraja works justice by calling women from her own clan but does not compromise on her power. She normalizes her position of supremacy but eventually, she does not realize that her interests and needs are indeed modified by culture. Fetishism is one of Madraja's attributes. She looks at people with utilitarian value. Madraja equates the five women with 'value' (exchange value) like properties or things. "Madraja was praising their legs, shoulders, arms. They were young, it's true. But with bodies used to hard work."(Devi 3)

Godhumi and her companions are a proletariat group who work together. They go to the palace only with the understanding that they will be Uttara's companions and not as Dasis. For the women to have a dialogue with Madraja based on such grounds, it is evident that they have passed the stages of domination, oppression, resistance, and exploitation of labor. Paulo Freire in his *Pedagogy of the Oppressed* talks about the peasant revolution, in which he says that the "peasants were never drunk or lazy, but they were exploited!" (Freire 64) By walking away from the royal palace once their land was quenched by the cool rainwater so that life could go on without disrupting the order of nature, the women freed themselves and escaped from exploitation. The Rajavritta Queens in Hastinapur is not free enough to see the happiness and freedom that the lokavritta women enjoy, yet they are not ready to give up their position of royalty. From the older Queen to the youngest, they are ready to wear the mask of 'being' a rajavritta by sacrificing their sons and husbands, eventually lives and the purpose of living. In this sense, the rajavritta women are deprived of happiness. They sacrifice everything for the sake of war. So, they become the subalterns as well. As Gayatri Spivak puts it in her chapter of *Collectivities* from *Death of a Discipline*, "Women are not a special case but can represent the asymmetries attendant upon any such representation." (70) Therefore, the concept of subalternity itself is gendered. In the little narrative of, *After Kurukshetra* that Mahasweta Devi had created, the author not only chose to see from the perspective of the marginalized, but also shows the treatment of women belonging to all classes from a subaltern eye.

The Chandals who are mentioned in the initial part of the story possess what is called the "Subaltern Mentality". Gautam Bhadra in his essay, *The Mentality of Subalternity: Kantanama or Rajdharma* says "Submissiveness to authority in one context is as frequent as defiance in another. It is these two elements (submissiveness and defiance) that constitute the subaltern mentality." (Bhadra 63). The Chandals don't partake in the war, but their job is to collect firewood and "quench the countless fires of the nameless dead with water." (Devi 2) This group of people has time and again accepted the dominance and exploitation and never tried to voice out or rebel. By bringing in the 'prostitute center' and the 'chandals' and placing them on the same platform, the author shows a meticulous shift in the center by the striking contrast between the Grand narrative and the Little narrative and how this sect of people are brought in the context of subaltern writing. An 'organic crisis' is seen here between civil society and the political society which lead to the Gramscian concept of hegemony. Hegemony occurs when either one of the 'base' or the 'superstructure' of the society fails to exercise power, while one group remains defiant and the other dominant. This part of the story of Chandals supports the concept of the theory of agency and subalternity.

In *Kunti and the Nishadin*, the authorial voice plays an important role in suggesting the prejudice and violence that take place while crossing borders. The rajavrittas have gotten used to the royal life. When they choose to live in the forest, the royal trio finds it difficult to understand the codes of nature: the birds, trees, wind, the nishads, etc. On the other hand when the Nishadins, not of their free will but who were invited by Kunti, went to the lac palace only to get cruelly burnt to ashes. Mahasweta Devi has pointed out some clear binary distinctions between Kunti and the Nishadins. Even in the basic act of collecting firewood, Kunti "drags" it back to the ashram whereas the Nishadins heft the bundles onto their heads. Kunti is weak and withered, carrying her burden of confessions. In contrast to them, the Nishadins "seems to be tranquil, happy, hardworking lot, their faces always wreathed in bright smiles" (Devi 28).

The collective consciousness of the subaltern (Nishadins) works against Kunti when she enters the forest. Both the groups fail to accommodate themselves in each other's space. Barbaric attempts at such a civilizational struggle end up nowhere but destruction. The Nishadins as well as Kunti, yearn for recognition, a recognition that would make the past wrongs partially disappear as a consolation. To quote Walter Benjamin from the book, *Walter Benjamin and History* by Andrew Benjamin, "Under its 'historical index' each Now is marked as the Now of another Now, and ... untouchable by that other Now, in which it is supposed to be recognized." (Benjamin 58) Kunti is in a very unstable position. She takes pride in being a Rajavritta but finds solace in the forest. She does not let go of her "colonizer mentality" and at the same time has a self-depreciative attitude which the subalterns possess. Her coupled personality overlaps with each other and pulls her down to disillusion. She seeks freedom from the overloaded responsibility as a queen of rajavritta. While trying to find peace in the forest, she sees the Nishads and she wants to be like them, carefree and happy. She tries to seize it but fails. This is very similar to the bourgeois structure of social relation, where co-operation or co-existence does not exist. In the case of Kunti and the Nishadin, it is the bourgeois class that struggles against the feudal force (Nishadins). A Necrophilic behavior: the destruction of life their own or that of their oppressed fellows are seen in Kunti, Gandhari, and Dritarashtra. The fact that they wait for the forest fire to consume them and Kunti's complete erasure of the memory of killing six nishadins in the lac palace reaffirms this point.

As Spivak mentions in her text *Death of a Discipline*, "Subaltern aboriginal groups read "nature" with uncanny precision. The weather predictions, altogether confine in geographical scope, are always astonishing to someone less used to living in the eco-biome."(Spivak 68) This is exactly what happens with Kunti in the forest because the forest life, the flora, and the fauna, and the nishad's culture is completely alien to her. She does not understand the honour of life, which is evident from her confessions of abandoning Karna immediately after his birth as well as in her stone reaction after Karna's death. Gandhari wept for Karna, Kunti did not. Kunti goes numb when she sees that the Nishadins had understood whatever she had spoken. Once the revelation had happened, there is a noticeable shift in the tone of language the Nishadins use. It is the tone of anger.

> I? Against the lokavritta? ...
>
> Let me jog your memory.
>
> You stayed there, in the house of lac, Jatugriha?
>
> Yes, it was a plot by Duryodhana…
>
> A scheme, right?A cruel plot?

Only the rajavritta can do such a thing. You live there for one year, knowing full well that the place will be burned to ashes, that you have to save yourself and your sons. You had to provide irrefutable proof that the six of you had been burned to death" (Devi 41).

The author lets the reader know the mind of Kunti. Initially, Devi seems to be sympathetic towards Kunti, describing her helpless position as a rajavritta. Kunti had been serving the Gods and the Brahmans all her life, in the middle of which a 'minor' incident like the plot for the six nishadins slip her mind. Nishadins know the language of Kunti. They are angry because she forgot to mention the cruel plot against the six nishadins in her long dramatic monologue of confessions. Mahasweta Devi's use of language is subtle, in a way that suggests Kunti's non-existent eye towards the nishadins. Kunti does not explicitly express her thoughts on the Nishadins, but the author subtly weaves them through her language.

The societies of the rajavritta were fully built on violent coercion where they are under an illusion that anybody other than their needs to be suppressed. When that fails and the opposing group fights back to regain their 'recognized' position, the problem arises within both classes. The subalterns are in a position of oscillation where at first they are in a normal position, after which they get suppressed by the bourgeoisie due to various class/caste/occupational differences, and then come to a stage where they fight back. In all three stories, the five women, Nishadins, Souvali, and Souvalya are in the last stage of oscillation and the return in the oscillatory movement makes the rajavrittas the subalterns. As Derrida in his "Structure, sign and play in the discourse of human sciences" says that, "the Centre is not the centre", it keeps shifting. The Grand narrative had the Kings and the Queen as their centre and in Subaltern writing, the common man becomes the centre.

The third story in the series gives a vibrant description of the protagonist Souvali. She is described as an "ageing woman, but still, a long plait. Black Choli. Green ghagra, yellow chunni…" (Devi 45) Devi has portrayed Souvali as a 'new woman' who is far away from the indigenous traditions. Souvali is an active agent in a society of change. But it is also undeniable that the mindset and attitude towards people who belong to a lower class than themselves remain the same until the 'other' group fights back. There is a passing reference of impurity towards the chandals, where Souvali tells her son to wash his feet before entering the house. The notion of untouchability and impurity of the lower class is seen as something universally internalized. Souvali is a story of the conflict between change and tradition. Devi has shown cultural osmosis in Indian society as highly complex. The anthropological and cultural difference in the imaginary man-made boundaries has come to a stage where it is seen as a farce when there had been a political disaster. The past after so many years has caught up with the present with Dhritarashtra, Gandhari, and Kunti. After the Mahatarpan, the people in the village talk about it as a mockery, "what happened today was such a mockery, wasn't it? ...Ahana and Varunya have gone to see the fun and games." (Devi 47)

Dhritarashtra is seen as an epitome of patriarchal dominance in the world of the rajavrittas. He begets a child and fails to acknowledge him as his son and fails to acknowledge the mother of this child (Souvali and Souvalya). Subalternity as a gendered concept creeps in again as a different aspect in the home/world dichotomy. Home as a space for women and the world for men is pointed out in the story. Souvali says "This is the only place where I can breathe freely."(Devi 47) Partha Chatterjee in his essay called *The Nation and its Women*, says, " The home in its essence must remain unaffected by the profane activities of the material world - and women are its representation… and so one gets an identification of social roles by gender to correspond with the separation of the social space into ghar and bahir."(Chatterjee 245) Chatterjee proposes a new meaning of the home/world dichotomy by saying, "with the identification of social roles by gender, we get the ideological framework within which nationalism answered the women's question." (Chatterjee 246) Souvali as a 'new' woman is quite the reverse of the 'common' women, "who was coarse, vulgar, loud, quarrelsome, devoid of superior moral sense, sexually promiscuous and a subject to brutal physical oppression by males."(Chatterjee 253) Souvali on the contrary expiates herself among the group of dasi women from the clutches of the rajavrittas so that she could wait for her long-lost son in her own house. Souvali says to the head dasi Dhruva, "I'm going to live on the outskirts of town."(49)

Uma Chakravarti in her essay entitled, *Whatever Happened to the Vedic Dasi?* Says, "The indigenous intelligentsias' were not functioning within a political and social vacuum. The natives were no passive recipients of the perception of the past, then in the process of being reconstituted." (Chakravarti 32) She also says that the indigenous literati were active agents in constructing the past and constantly engaged in choosing the embryonic body of knowledge from current social and political concerns. In all the three stories of Mahasweta Devi, the so-called subaltern women have played the role of asserting their identity despite all odds. In the larger picture of marga tradition, which is positioned in a horizontal scale and the desi traditional people, especially women, who are vertically positioned, get disappeared under the greater shadow. Since no one notices their existence, it is natural that there was no one to mourn for their disappearance in the Grand Narrative. The transition from the grand narrative to the little narrative has missed out to produce an organic unity because it never existed in any society. In subaltern writing, the theorists and writers are not criticizing the traditions. But they are trying to focus on the left out aspects of the society, which needs to be given a voice so that there can be a mutual understanding between all people. Beyond the division of class, caste, and gender discrimination, Mahasweta Devi through her collection of stories like *After Kurukshetra*, *Imaginary Maps*, and various other writings, is trying to give her readers a message to look at people as humans and not with discriminatory codes. The aspect of Agency and Subalternity in Mahasweta Devi's *After Kurukshetra*, in this chapter has focused mainly on women as subalterns, be it the rajavrittas or the lokavrittas. Despite attaining the position of royalty, the rajavritta women are still struggling to assert their individuality despite the lokavritta women's success in regaining their rightful status. Their higher status in society has created a hindrance to their individualism.

References:

Benjamin, Andrew. *Walter Benjamin and History*. London: Continuum, 2005.

Chatterjee, Partha. "The Nation and its Women". *A Subaltern Studies Reader*. Ed. Ranajit Guha. New Delhi: OUP, 1997.

Chakravarti, Uma. "Whatever Happened to the Vedic Dasi?" *Recasting Women*. Ed. Kumkum Sangari and Sudesh Vaid. New Delhi: Kali for Women, 1989.

Derrida, Jacques. "Structure, Sign and Play in the Discourse of Human Sciences" *Writing and Difference*, trans. Allan Bass. London: Routledge, 1978.

Devi, Mahasweta. *After Kurukshetra.* Trans. Anjum Katyal. Calcutta: Seagull books, 2005.

Masjids and Architecture: New Spiritual Spatiality of Muslims in Kerala

Anfal. M

The concern and consciousness of people are aesthetically represented in the spatial architecture they build. The mind and space of humans are drawn to a familiar or desirous world of their own. With these spatial ideas in mind, I am searching in this paper for orientation of Muslim spatial identities in Kerala especially by focusing upon the architectural turn of Masjids in Kerala built after gulf migrations of Muslims in the state. As remittances, mainly from Gulf countries, flowed to Kerala in the 1970s and 80s, the state began to watch newly designed Masjids. Different from the Kerala model of traditional architecture, many newly built Masjids in the state show distinguished architectural beauty and elegance. Carried away by the fact that Masjids are built as spiritual and prayer centres for Muslims, the recent tendency of Masjids being constructed in new structures and architectures hints towards a paramount change in the spatial orientation of Muslims in the state. An analysis of architectural varieties of those Masjids leads considerably to the theoretical framework of the spiritual spatiality of Muslims in Kerala. For better understanding, I have selected two Masjids from different regions recently built in the state. To explore this topic theoretically, I have selected a theoretical concept "Architecture of Enjoyment" coined by the French philosopher Henry Lefebvre. My argument is that a synesthetic form of jouissance that combines both spiritual elevation and bodily pleasure could be applied to the architectural designs and structures of newly built Masjids in Kerala.

Throughout history, the spatial orientation of a place is naturally reflected in its dwelling spaces and buildings. The concern and consciousness of people are aesthetically represented in the spatial architecture they build as well. "We are spatially never simply here present as objects taking up space, but rather we are "there" where our concerns are, and we understand ourselves in terms of those spatial projections by which we overcome distance and, in our nearness to things, we take up a place. To take up a place is to be with things as those which concern us" (Murchadha 28). Human beings have, thus, a tempted orientation in their mind and space towards a familiar or desirous world of them.

The background to this chapter is primarily my interest to search for spatial orientation of Muslim identities in Kerala especially after I read a 1987 published article in *India Today* titled "Mosques Sprout All Over in Kerala, in a Variety of Shapes". As the article narrated the emergence of newly shaped and designed

Masjids in Kerala, my focus is upon the architectural turn of Masjids in Kerala after the Gulf migrations of Muslims in the state. In the 1970s and 1980s, Kerala Muslims were introduced to newly constructed Masjids, using remittances from Gulf countries. Masjids were constructed on a large scale, as the article stated that "it is impossible to miss them on the 650-km drive from Trivandrum in southern Kerala to Kasargod in the north. Round every second bend, the minarets of a gleaming new mosque reach for the sky. Unexpectedly, Kerala's skyline is changing" (Pillai Para 1).

Post-1970s, Kerala, especially Malabar, witnessed the unprecedented flow of Gulf source remittance and it got reflected in the region's economic and socio-cultural platforms. The influence that the relocation and the remittances have had on the socio-cultural conversion of Muslims in Kerala more than on any other cultural and religious groups in the state has been due to many reasons. Most importantly, a great portion of total expatriates has been the populace from the Muslim community.

For example, according to the census of 2001, Muslims constitute less than a quarter (24.7 percentage) of the total population in Kerala (Census of India 2001, Kerala), although their proportion is doubled among the emigrants. A study by CDS, Trivandrum, estimated that the total migrant population from Kerala in the Gulf was 18.48 lakh in 2007, of which 8.83 lakh were Mappila Muslims. In 2004 and 1999, the share of migrant population of Mappila Muslims was 43.7 and 41.9 percentage respectively" (Kurian 2002).

The specificity of socio-economic circumstances of Muslims in the state along with the cultural, ethnic, and religious relations of the community to the Arab countries to where they migrated helped them to develop both economically and socially. Also, the spiritual ideologies along with the cultural and social identities that Muslims carried out and brought from the Gulf countries to their native place were on par with the economic prosperity they attained because of the migration. The already inherent strong religious background of Kerala Muslims in the state kept with the Arab merchants for centuries and also by the religious preaching made by Arabs, along with the strong religious learning system in the state, is the influential constituents in moulding the lives of Kerala Muslims.

The structure of Masjids in the earliest time of arrival of Islam in Arabia was quiet in a simple form. "In the beginning mosque structure was quite simple. The genesis of the mosque is found in the house constructed by the Prophet after his exile from Mecca. It was a large enclosure with an open portico at one end and roofed with palm leaves. It had neither a dome nor minarets and cloisters". (Mosque Architecture Para.3) Later on in India, varied Indian styles and forms were combined and blended with features of Islamic architecture. Religious monuments and Masjids in the country were given a form of these synthesized architectural structures.

Islamic architecture has evolved from a synthesis of various styles prevalent in different Islamic countries. Indian indigenous style of architecture was different both in form and spirit which is required for a mosque. This conflict prevailed in the first phase of design and construction of mosques in India, but gradually overcome this difficulty through a blend of two different styles and evolved the Indo-Islamic architecture (Mosque Architecture Para.5)

However, in Kerala, the architecture of Masjids was based neither on the Arabic nor Indo-Islamic forms. Instead, the architecture of Masjids built in the earlier time in Kerala was rigidly based on the tradition of the region.

They are simple buildings with tiled roofs, large prayer halls covered verandah all around, tall basements, walls made of laterite blocks... Early mosques in Kasaragod and Kannur districts show the influence of the Jain style of architecture. The Thalankara mosque was an old Jain Basthi. Certain mosques in Kannur show two different styles with Indo-Saracenic elements with the minarets and British colonial style with double cylindrical pillows, large windows, etc. (Mosque Architecture Para.6)

Different from the Kerala model of traditional architecture, many newly built Masjids in the state show distinguished architectural beauty and elegance. Carried away by the fact that Masjids are built as spiritual and prayer centres for Muslims, the recent tendency of Masjids being constructed in new structures and architectures hints towards a paramount change in the spatial orientation of Muslims in the state. An analysis of architectural varieties of those Masjids leads considerably to the theoretical framework of the spiritual spatiality of Muslims in Kerala.

Masjids and Architectural Jouissance:

A theoretical concept of architectural varieties used among recently built Masjids in Kerala can be connected with what the spatial theorist Henry Lefebvre termed as the architecture of enjoyment. Lefebvre's approach toward the architectural analysis, which he explained in his 1973 published work *Versune Architecture de Jouissance,* translated as *Towards an Architecture of Enjoyment*, contains a multidisciplinary analysis of public and private buildings and their architectural affiliations. Chiefly associated with the concept of jouissance, translated as pleasure, and describing the vivid aspects of "enjoyment," "contentment," "satisfaction," "bliss."(Bononno viii) The book describes that "something like the architecture of enjoyment is only possible within a total revolution of social conditions. So, in a way, architecture of enjoyment is both possible and impossible. It is possible if society changes; it is impossible otherwise. Architecture is, of course, part of society, so it could be part of an overall change in the material conditions of existence, but it is not in and of itself a way to change society in a revolutionary way." (Gamsby 80)

A large portion of contemporary built Masjids in Kerala are designed, arguably, according to Arabian architectural designs thanks to the changing or already changed social conditions of Muslim living in the state. That is to say, the impact of Arabian nations, owing to the large influence of Gulf immigration among the Muslims in the state and the resultant flow of money into the state, created a revolutionary state of Muslim life, especially in Malabar, and it is reflected in overall mentality and activities of them. Naturally, that shift from the traditional attitudes and mentalities paved the way to an exclusive feeling of jouissance, as Lefebvre described it, contained with the spiritual mentality of local Muslims when newly designed Masjids appeared their lands. Even three decades before, this tendency started to emerge. Writing about new prayer centres built in the 1980s in his article, Sreedhar Pillai stated that "the new mosques stand out in Kerala's verdant countryside. Opulent and garish, they resemble the sprawling multi-coloured mansions of the nouveau riche Malayalees who found work in the Gulf." (Pillai Para 3) A fresh sensual pleasure bounded with spiritual satisfaction by watching out or praying in these Arabian architectural edifices was arguably experienced by this group. Here the imaginary presence of an Arabian aura, which is sacred from an Islamic perspective, along with the long before-started attraction of Kerala Muslims to those countries is imbibed in the minds of the mass connected with those Masjids. Architecture, in this context, turns out to be something more than its physical presence. As Lefebvre specified the architecture in *Towards an Architecture of Enjoyment* as a condition of imaging more than a specific process or a group of monuments, these Masjids are viewed as an architecture of jouissance—of delight or pleasure—focused on the body and its internal beats and founded on the existence of the senses.

To explain this phenomenon more clearly, I opted for two Masjids from different regions built recently in the state. One is 2010 built Ma'din Grand Masjid at Malappuram in the Malabar region and the second is Muhyudheen Juma Masjid opened for prayer in 2019 at Nattika in Thrissur district of the state. An aesthetical and critical observation of the architectural and spatial analysis of these two Masjids by understanding their social and spiritual importance will give what Lefebvre stated as sensual *jouissance.*

The prayer hall inside Nattika Muhiyudheen Juma Masjid (Panopics) apart from the comparatively architectural grandeur these Masjids offer which consciously adds to a sensual joy while watching the building or praying inside it, there is a strong element of spiritual aura that causes a sensual joy for the people who experience these spaces. The architectural structure of the prayer hall, for instance, the interior design of the prayer hall or the outer view of a Minaret, is not at all the cause of a bodily pleasure when a person is involved in spiritual activities or when his/her mind is spiritually overwhelmed. According to Lefebvre, the authentic pleasure is absent or removed from the heart when the consciousness of space is entered into the person's mind.

There is an important admonition; however, the architecture will never magically generate enjoyment in and of itself. Lefebvre is hostile to such fetishistic spatial reductionism, for enjoyment can emerge from anywhere precisely because of its elusive, bodily, fleeting nature (an abandoned warehouse, he says, can be quickly turned into a place of celebration). Further, if the goal of creating "a space of enjoyment" becomes too explicit and spatially fixed, genuine enjoyment is destroyed. In a particularly important section, Lefebvre writes that "the places of enjoyment" should not have pleasure or sensuality "as their function" (Gordillo Para. 10).

In this context, though the presence of Arabian architectural forms imparted into the two Masjids detailed above may add sensual joy among devotees connected with those Masjids, there is the fear of loss of bodily pleasure acquired with their spiritual consciousness. Lefebvre discusses this clash very clearly: "Spaces of enjoyment cannot consist of a building, an assembly of rooms, places determined by their functions" (Lefebvre 152). Rather, they emerge through bodies expending their vital energies in "moments, encounters, friendships, festivals, rest, quiet, joy, exaltation, sensuality, as well as understanding, enigma, the unknown, and the known, struggle, play"(152).

But here in the case of the Masjids, there arises a synthesized form of *jouissance.* One is bodily pleasure accompanied by the spiritual elevation of a devotee at a prayer hall of the Masjids either by taking part in the prayer or by being present in that spiritual atmosphere. The second one is the sensual experience of the devotee by watching the Arabian architectural elements carved into the prayer space. He enters into that imaginary Arabian space and performs the prayer. As Lefebvre stated, "every time you find a place genuinely pleasing and enchanting… you enter this utopia" (132).and acquire the exalted joy combined with both bodily and sensual pleasures. The architecture of the Masjids is elevated here into an all-embracing element of human enjoyment both imaginarily and spiritually.

Symbolic and Analogical Functions of Masjids:

What do the architectures of these Masjids symbolically or analogically convey? The architectures can be classified into Symbolic and Analogical architectures.

The symbolic object can differ in endless ways from what it symbolizes and, yet, correspond to it through an encoded magical and mystical connection. Thus, an upright stone symbolizes constancy, force, virility, propriety. It is a part of a whole, which that part reflects or designates. The analogical, on the other hand, reproduce, at least partially or apparently, the principle it claims to represent. It is based on clearly represented similarities. The symbol could be compared with metonymy and the analogy with metaphor (Lefebvre 144).

Generally categorized, the constituents in a Masjid are four types.

The most common, found in all types of mosques throughout history, refers to "paradise." The second, … "the heavenly theatre", … related to the unique function of the mosque as the place for communal prayer … third, mosques are often understood as "urban sculptures that guide visitors through the cities…(and) "the cosmic spiral" is the final symbol that is common to many structures, forms, and decorations in the Islamic world and relates to a medieval understanding of time and space"(Erzen 126).

Since Masjids commonly represent many spiritual, social, and cosmic meanings through their architectural and symbolic formations, a deep observation of those components helps to understand what devotees or people who experience it gain or understand from these spaces.

The Islamic view of the world, within which the architecture of the mosque developed, is influenced by a sense of adoration for the creations of God. Such adoration renders everything with the emotion of love, leading to empathy and giving rise to an aesthetic relation to the world. Consequently, all Islamic artworks, including Islamic architecture and specifically the architecture of mosques, need to be understood and appraised in terms of the symbols that are embodied therein (Erzen 126).

The above statements about the architectural space in Islam denote that the base for the creation of every architectural work, be they monuments or buildings including Masjids or calligraphic works, is love and empathy. Further, the symbolic components related to the Masjids, for example, the Masjids discussed above, would add some of their meanings when the context of their construction is changed. That is, in Islamic architecture, no matter how much a building confirms to a set, a preexisting plan, its final form will vary according to the actual conditions of site, topography, patron, and local traditions. Moreover, buildings will be designed to be appreciated as they undergo constantly changing conditions which daily and annually produce changes of mood and atmosphere' (Erzen 130).

This change in the mood and atmosphere is what would be reflected in the case of two Masjids described in this work. Apart from the spiritual and religious aura in the architecture and formation of these two prayer centres through their symbolic and analogical components, their exclusive meanings imparted here, while observing the context and background of their creations, are unique and more complex.

The glory of Arabian lands in spiritual and economic platforms have immensely impacted the view of Kerala Muslims in building Masjids with architectures and symbolic and aesthetical concepts indebted from lands of the earlier. The structures of both Ma'din and Muhyudheen Masjids in outer view, which are unfamiliar to traditional architectural styles used for the earlier Masjids in the state, resemble that of an Arabian edifice by arguably offering devotees an aura that they are at a Masjid in an Arabian region. It could be the result of a deep connection that this community has been keeping with Arabian lands. The structure of minarets, domes and Mimbers, arch-shaped entrances, larger emptied prayer halls, design of outer structures and beautification of the interior and exterior spaces, settings of the lights and artworks in Arabian styles, etc. pass to these people a symbolic and analogical meaning in confluence with an Arabian charisma. Mental mapping of Arabian space and its architecture helps in a great way for this imaginary realization.

The above analysis proves that the influence of the Arab world in the life and culture of Muslims in Kerala has not only been visible in its outer spheres. Rather, it points out that the latter is deeply in touch with the aesthetical and even spiritual realm of the earlier as the cases of the architecture studies of these two Masjids portray in their altered social and cultural setting. It proves that human beings have a stimulated emplacement of their mind and space towards either an acquainted or wishful world related to them.

References:

Bononno, Robert. Translator's Note, *Toward an Architecture* of Enjoyment. New York: University of Minnesota, 2014.

Erzen, JaleNejdet. "Reading Mosques: Meaning and Architecture in Islam." *The Journal of Aesthetics and Art Criticism*, Vol. 69, no. 1, (2011).

JSTOR, www.jstor.org/stable/42635843. Accessed 18 Jan. 2020.

Gamsby, Patrick. *The Canadian Journal of Sociology / Cahiers Canadiens De Sociology*, Vol. 40, no.1(2015). JSTOR, www.jstor.org/stable/canajsocicahican.40.1.79.Accessed 14 Jan. 2020..

Lefebvre, Henri. *Towards an Architecture of Enjoyment.* Edited Lukasz Stanek, UMP, 2014.

Social Class and Individualism in Aravind Adiga's *The White Tiger*

S. Keerthana

Aravind Adiga is a contemporary Indian writer who writes in English. He wrote the famous work *The White Tiger* which was awarded the Man Booker prize in 2008. Adiga deals with many ideas and concepts in this novel like corruption, individualism, injustice, poor and rich dominance, etc. The main theme of the novel is the contrast between India's rise as a modern global economy and its working-class people who live in crushing poverty. The white tiger in the novel deals with the protagonist's struggle to establish themselves in a hostile social environment and the decline of traditional culture under the impact of westernization. The novel provides a darkly humorous perspective of India's class struggle in a globalized world as told through a retrospective narration from Balram Halwai, a village boy who journeys from the darkness of village life to the life of entrepreneurial success in an utterly amoral, brilliantly irreverent, deeply endearing and altogether unforgettable manner. The language used is coherent and spontaneous. The white tiger has been hailed as an "incredible trip into the dazzling and pulsating heart of India" through the emergence of Balram from the India of Darkness to the India of Light. This paper deals with sociological aspects in the novel *The White Tiger.*

Literature is created from painful and pleasant memories and experiences of history. Writing is evidence of the writers' tremendous power and evolution, which plays an effective means to express the colossal human problems in a wide context. Aravind Adiga's debut novel, the coveted Man Booker Prize-Winning, *The White Tiger* opens "a Pandora box, unleashing ugliness, beauty, misery, and brilliance

From the general to the particular, Balram admits that he is a "half-baked" India like thousands of others in India, for he hasn't had a proper school education and he is self-educated; he has been overhearing the conversations of others that his school has been "the road and the pavement". He ought, therefore to call his story, The Autobiography of a Half-Baked Indian,

Me, and thousands of others in this country like me, are half-baked because we are never allowed *to complete our schooling.*

The basic facts about Balram, his "origin, height, weight, known sexual deviations, etc." are all listed in the poster issued by the police proclaiming him a criminal when he escapes from Delhi after having murdered his employer Ashok. He hasn't been recognized so far because the photograph on the poster resembles most men from the India of Darkness.

Laxmangarh is the exact opposite of what a "typical Indian Village paradise" should be. It has no electricity, no water supply, and no means of communication with the outside world.

Delhi opens a new world to Balram, it is the India of Light the capital of a modern global economy – where the rich zoom around in their egg-shelled cars which only crack open to let a bejewelled hand of a lady throw an empty mineral bottle into the street. Balram narrates the story of his life to the visiting Chinese Premier through e-mail by telling him that "India is two countries in one: an India of Light, and an India of Darkness". He was born in the village of Laxmangarh in Gaya District (Bihar) into a larger family on the banks of "Mother Ganga, daughter of the Vedas, a river of illumination, protector of us all, breaker of the chain of birth and rebirth", adding, "Everywhere this river flows, that area is the Darkness". Despite their grinding poverty and oppressive living conditions, the people are religious; they accept their perpetual servitude to landlords and politicians as something ingrained in their psyche and can't even think of betraying their masters for fear of the dire consequences that would destroy their families.

The motif of light and darkness appears all through the narrative of *The White Tiger*. For the protagonist, Balram Halwai, the river Ganga is the symbol of darkness. The representatives of light and darkness are India's cities and villages. In the countryside, ruled by darkness, the name, family, caste, and religion mean everything to people. But all these distinctions disappear in the cities, where people are either rich or poor. Taking up another job than what caste allows is and trying to dilute the case. Balram has often bribed the officer earlier to get out of trouble and he is his "scum" when the boy wants to file an FIR against Balram, the corrupt assistant commissioner glibly advises him to go home and come back the next morning when the FIR will be filled

Balram, the protagonist of the novel, comes from the lowest of the low Halwai caste in Laxmangarh, a backward village in Gaya District, Bihar. While the rest of the men-folk from his large family presided over by the matriarch Kusum Granny, have either left for Dhanbad, Calcutta, or Delhi in search of job or work in the fields owned by the landlord nicknamed frowned upon and not tolerated in the India of Darkness.

Balram is given another name, the White Tiger, by the visiting school inspector who is impressed by his talent and intelligence. But his school days soon come to an end because he is made to join a tea shop along with his elder brother Kishan to pay off debts incurred for a cousin's dowry. It is while working as a "human spider" at the tea shop that Balram gets what he calls his real education. He is punished and dismissed by the tea shop owner. It is at the tea shop that he gets his birthday, courtesy of the ensuing elections when every young man turns eighteen is declared eligible to vote.

Balram and his family belong to the lowest caste, Halwai so they are doomed to live in utter poverty and destitution; they work in the fields belonging to the high-caste landlords and "swallow their daily wages", Balram's father, Vikram Halwai, a self-respecting rickshaw-puller, has a "plan" for his son by sending him to the village school, while his elder brother as a "human spider" in the village tea shop. But he continues his education by eavesdropping on and overhearing the customer's conversation for which he is punished and dismissed by the tea shop owner.

Corruption, however, is rampant in India that the author describes. It is a fact of life that every Indian has to love. This reflects in "the model Indian village paradise" which lacks the basic infrastructure- education, communications, nutrition, running water, sanitation, and healthcare- facilities that are easily available in a metropolis like Delhi.

Balram compares the plight of the poor to chickens living in a rooster coop in the poultry market. Perpetual servitude to their masters is so deeply ingrained in their psyche that they can't even think of rebelling. Balram is an exceptional case, the proverbial White Tiger, a rare species who breaks out of the rooster coop to emerge from the India of Darkness to the India of Light at considerable risk to his family back home in Laxmangarh. He belongs to the 99.9 percent of Indians and in the White Tiger, he narrates how he was corrupted by life in the city "from a sweet innocent village fool into a citified fellow full of debauchery, depravity, and wickedness". This is a stinging comment on the situation prevailing in India. Yet Balram exults in his success:

I've made it! I've broken out of the coop!

I've given myself away.

Breaking the law of the land, he says, is "the entrepreneur's prerogative" because he was "not destined to be a slave" all his life. Balram is just not free in India. So there is just one chance to be free; to be your own master, which he now is.

A small branch of "Mother Ganga, daughter of the Vedas, river in illumination, protector of us all, breaker of the chain of birth and rebirth," flows just outside Laxmangarh, which is cut off from the rest of the world. Balram advises the visiting Chinese Premier "not to dip in the Ganga unless you want your mouth full of faces, straw, soggy parts of human bodies, buffalo carrion, and seven different kinds of industrial acids." "Everywhere this river flows, that area is the Darkness." It was on the banks of this holy river that Balram's mother was cremated when he was seven or eight years of age.

The White Tiger chronicles harsh truths about present-day India within the framework of an absorbing novel. It is "an intelligent and ruthless portrait of India in the marking –shining or rising, but always sinking", its appeal comes from a "total lack of sentimentally and the consequent realism it thus manages" in portraying and the consequent realism it thus manages" in portraying a vivid India, even though it may be gritty, bitter, sardonic, and nasty.

At the end of his self-confession to Mr. Jiabao, Balram justifies his murder by saying, "I will never say I made a mistake when I slit my master's throat that night in Delhi. To know what it means not to be a servant, even for a day, hour, or minute, was worth everything in the world to me".

References:

Aravind Adiga. *The White Tiger: A Freakish Booker.* New Delhi: Authors Press, 2011.

Nagpal, Pratibha. *Aravind Adiga's The White Tiger: A Critical Response.* Ed. R.K Dhawan. New Delhi: Prestige Books, 2009.

A Metamodern Analysis of Moral Ambiguity through the Books and Web Series: 'A Series of Unfortunate Events'

Khadija Begum

Metamodernism is a recent and amorphous cultural and theoretical concept. It is being increasingly understood in one of the two ways. Either it is understood to be the negation of the skepticism and nihilism of postmodernism or a return to the safe illusion of positivity of modernism. However, Jason Ananda Jospehson-Storm points out that the prefix, "meta," suggests, "… a higher- or second-order position beyond (post) modernism." Therefore, metamodernism cannot be discussed without a complete understanding of the consequences of postmodernism. To illustrate the approach and method of enquiry of postmodernism, and how metamodernism goes beyond it, I have chosen the book and web series, "A Series of Unfortunate Events." In the context of "A Series of Unfortunate Events," these two movements influenced the events themselves and how they are portrayed.

The book series leans more into postmodernism while being aware of its shortcomings and tries to go beyond it.

However, it is the web series that welcomes the possibilities metamodernism promises. Overall, "A Series of Unfortunate Events" embodies both postmodern and metamodern features in its exploration of themes such as loss, trauma, morality, and the search for meaning in a chaotic world. I have chosen the character Count Olaf, that stands for moral ambiguity in the contemporary culture, as the focus of my analyses to demonstrate how the theory of metamodernism can bring forth clarity or the solution we might seek for the problems that the methods of postmodernism cannot seem to solve.

"A Series of Unfortunate Events" began with a fire that destroyed the protagonists' (Violet, Sunny, Klaus) home, killing their parents. This event can be seen as postmodern in the way that it challenges traditional ideas of safety, security, and stability. The protagonists are forced to navigate a chaotic and unpredictable world where they can no longer rely on the structures and institutions that were supposed to protect them.

As the story progresses, the protagonists are subjected to a series of unfortunate events that further destabilize their sense of self and reality. These events represent a tug of war between metamodern and postmodern in the way that they explore both irony and sincerity, cynicism and hopefulness, and complexity and simplicity. The story challenges the reader's assumptions and forces them to question their understanding of the world.

Postmodernism, altered the course of many fields of human sciences but not entirely productively. Postmodernism is characterized by a rejection of objective truth, grand narratives, and traditional forms of authority. While it had a significant impact on many areas of culture and thought, including art, literature, and philosophy, it has also been subject to criticism and critique from a variety of perspectives.

A critique of postmodernism is its tendency towards deconstruction and criticism, without offering any solutions or alternatives. Postmodernism is good at exposing problems and flaws in existing systems. Throughout the series, the guardians in "A Series of Unfortunate Events" are a commentary on the ways in which power and influence operate in society, and how these dynamics can impact the lives of those who are subject to them. By presenting a range of different guardians with varying motives and values, the series encourages readers to think critically about the social structures that shape their own lives and the lives of others around them. While it is a necessary critique, it fails to provide a way to reach any meaningful alternatives or solutions.

Another key criticism of postmodernism is its rejection of objective truth and its embrace of relativism because it leads to a nihilistic worldview. Count Olaf reflects this when he says, "There is no good or bad, no right or wrong. There is only power, and those too weak to seek it." The nihilistic view can make the world seem as unpredictable and confusing, and individuals are often unable to reach meaning. Making it difficult to engage in meaningful dialogue or debate and to address important issues facing the world today.

Literary theorist and cultural critic Fredric Jameson, is one of the critics of postmodernism who has expressed concerns about the negative impact of postmodernism on cultural production. He argues that postmodernism's emphasis on fragmentation, pastiche, and the dissolution of the subject has led to a loss of critical agency and a retreat into cynicism and apathy. He says, "Postmodernism, as a cultural dominant, has had a tremendous impact on the way we think about and experience the world around us. It has shattered the grand narratives and utopian dreams of modernity, revealing the contradictions and limitations of our cultural and political institutions. At the same time, however, it has left us adrift in a sea of images, signs, and sounds, without the critical tools and discursive frameworks necessary to make sense of them. We are left with a sense of disorientation and disillusionment, unable to distinguish between reality and simulation, truth, and fiction, the authentic and the artificial."

No theory is without its flaws and limitations. While postmodernism's skepticism can be lauded for its zeal to question the very foundations of intellectual enquiry. It led humanities and social sciences to take a step back and evaluate its methods of enquiry along with its objects of enquiry. Which is not a bad thing in itself. While false positivism or misguided universalism may distract from postmodernism's ringing questions, they are not the solutions. For instance, The volunteers in "A Series of Unfortunate Events" who blindly follow authority and turn a blind eye to the bad in society are portrayed as victims of their own naivete and lack of critical thinking skills. They are nothing more than happiness pumps.

While postmodernism has been criticized for its relativism and skepticism, its concerns about power, diversity, and inclusion remain relevant and important today. In many ways, the issues that postmodernism sought to address continue to shape our contemporary cultural and political landscape. However, without a proper method, direction and motive of enquiry, there has been no way ahead. In a way, postmodernism has been counterproductive because it has not realized the full potential of the two methods it uses – deconstruction and subjectivity.

For instance, postmodernism's emphasis on subjectivity and interpretation through personal experience (which are grounds for relativism) can also be problematic in certain contexts, such as in the areas of science and medicine. This problem is well illustrated in the books and the web series through the character of Aunt Josephine. Aunt Josephine is extremely fearful and paranoid about everything, which causes her to misinterpret harmless situations as dangerous and ultimately puts the Baudelaire children in danger. For example, she is afraid of doorknobs because she believes they are unsanitary and could cause a disease, even though this can be based in reality but is far-fetched. Aunt Josephine's worldview is in contradiction to reality because her worldview informed by extreme fear and paranoia causes her to overlook actual dangers and makes her a liability to the Baudelaire children.

Postmodernism also made its method of deconstruction problematic. To get to the essence of an object, postmodernism used the method of deconstruction of the object. However, it did not lead to an understanding of the object, but it isolated the object and became more of an enigma than it ever was. For instance, postmodernism suggests that there is no objective truth, and that all truths are constructed through social and cultural processes. While this is a valuable insight, it can also lead to a situation where facts and evidence are dismissed as mere constructions, and where conspiracy theories and alternative facts can gain ground. For instance, "The Daily Punctilio" in the series distorts facts, spreads false information, sensationalizes news stories and sways public opinion about the Baudelaire children as it pleases.

Deconstruction is a great point to begin an intellectual enquiry as it informs us that individual perspectives or worldviews, social norm and cultural norms or political agendas can influence and construct social object like truth as they please. However, this conclusion reveals more about the factors acting upon the object rather than the object itself. Deconstruction, as it seeks to uncover the hidden assumptions and power structures, is ideal to clean the dust off of a social object and that's it. How do we study the object itself? This is where metamodernism comes in the picture.

Josephson argues that deconstructionism can be reconceptualized in the context of metamodernism. In the metamodernist perspective, deconstruction is not simply about undermining established power structures and challenging the status quo. It is not about accepting meaninglessness as the absolute truth rather; it is about creating new forms of meaning by discovering new vantage points. In other words, Josephson suggests that deconstruction can be used as a tool for reconstruction

An example of deconstruction and reconstruction in the "Series of Unfortunate Events" could be the portrayal of education and knowledge. Throughout the series, the concept of education is deconstructed through the Baudelaire children's experiences with their various guardians and the educational systems they encounter. It demonstrates how education, a mode/tool of knowledge, can negate the purpose of knowledge by routine memorization, heavy focus on measurements and data (represented by Prufrock Preparatory School) or following rigid rules and inadequate traditions (represented by the Village of Fowl Devotees). However, the books and web series also depict another mode of knowledge.

Books and libraries are a recurring motif throughout "A Series of Unfortunate Events." They are shown as a power, and refuge for the Baudelaire children. In many of the books, the children rely on books and libraries to solve mysteries and escape dangerous situations. For example, in "The Wide Window", the children use a library to research the mysterious "V.F.D." organization, and in "The Reptile Room," they find sanctuary in the library while being pursued by Count Olaf.

However, the author is aware that the books and libraries are yet another mode of education and just as vulnerable and fragile, easily destroyed or lost. This is exemplified by the burning of the V.F.D. library in "The Penultimate Peril," which represents the loss of knowledge and history. One tool defeats the purpose of knowledge and the other exemplifies it. Neither tell us what knowledge is. However, this useful exercise in deconstructing the portrayal of education and knowledge in "A Series of Unfortunate Events" challenges readers to think critically about the purpose and value of education, and encourages them to approach pursuit of knowledge in a more creative and independent manner. Thereby, laying down a strong foundation for reconstruction. Postmodernism's lack of substantial solutions can be more harmful than the benefit of its skepticism. But reconstruction through deconstruction is a method to get rid of an approach that creates loops upon loops. The best way to understand reconstruction would be to apply it.

The breakdown of morality in the recent times is plain to see. The rise of postmodernism has contributed to moral ambiguity. Postmodernism rejects the notion of absolute truth and instead sees reality as subjective and constantly shifting.

This perspective can make it difficult to determine what is right or wrong as there is no fixed standard against which to measure. The first step in reconstructive approach is to clean the dust off of the social object. So, let's deconstruct.

The history of morality is a long and complex one, spanning many centuries and cultures. At its core, morality is concerned with the distinction between right and wrong, good and bad, and the principles that guide human behavior. Over time, the concept of morality has evolved and transformed in response to changing social, cultural, and political contexts.

One of the earliest recorded systems of morality is found in the Code of Hammurabi in ancient Babylon around 1754 BCE. The code was based on justice and fairness. In ancient Greece, morality was based on virtues like courage and wisdom, which was seen as the key to living a good and fulfilling life. In the Judeo-Christian tradition, morality was based on divine commandments. God's will became the center of morality. During the Enlightenment period, morality was redefined in more secular terms, with thinkers such as Immanuel Kant emphasizing the importance of reason, autonomy, and universal moral principles.

However, the 20th century saw a growing skepticism towards universal moral principles and the idea of objective moral truth. This skepticism was fueled by a range of factors, including the horrors of World War II and the increasing cultural and political diversity of the postmodern era.

Postmodernism challenged the idea of objective moral truth, emphasizing instead the social construction of morality and the ways in which moral values and beliefs are shaped by power relations and cultural contexts.

The purpose of retracing the history of morality is to illustrate that morality like any other social phenomenon is constantly changing. Due to postmodernism's critique, it is revealed that at its very core morality is not universal. Over centuries, across continents different cultures have defined morality in varied ways. It has been socially constructed in a myriad of ways at different temporal and geographical moments. The problem is not what morality is inherently or the way it came to be. The question is not of it being real or unreal. If morality was truly ambiguous, indeterminable and subjective, it would have been easy to justify tyranny, oppression, or racism and there would have never been the need to get rid of them. Therefore, the real problem is what social processes morality has been subjected to throughout history.

Morality, a rather flexible social phenomenon, becomes a set of rigid rules when cultural norms and political purposes make it non-negotiable. This does not mean that morality is intrinsically a flawed concept. Anything of the world, be it socially occurring or naturally, will fall into the hands of other if not all areas of human life or dragged into a variety of contexts. Different individuals or societies will look at it with their own perspectives, that are shaped by their experiences. Exactly how it has been done with morality so far. Morality being flexible becomes a norm and its rigidity an exception. Moreover, this rigidity does not say anything about morality itself but more about the perspective or even the individual or society. What can we learn about morality if we choose to experience it through the factors acting upon it? However, these revelations about these different factors led postmodernism to declare morality futile instead of formulating another method to better understand morality. This conclusion is the direct result of the approach and method of scrutiny postmodernism choose. Through the lens of nihilism what would be even considered meaningful?

Let us try to understand what morality is through the tool of reconstruction with the approach to go beyond. Count Olaf's morality in "A Series of Unfortunate Events" is shaped by a variety of factors, including his upbringing, his personal experiences, and his desire for safety (represented by parents, siblings and friends) which he disguises as lust for wealth.

Olaf lost his mother to a mysterious fire and his father was accidentally killed by a close friend. The Baudelaire children too lose their noble parents to the treachery of the world. Olaf is portrayed as selfish, manipulative, and abusive, which may be due to the circumstances of his life. The Baudelaire children too increasingly begin to adopt morally questionable ways to outwit and defeat Count Olaf. They lie, they steel, they help commit arson even if their intentions were different from Count Olaf's.

They too, judging by the conventional mode of morality, are wrong. It turns out by the same measure their parents are not exactly noble as well.

Furthermore, despite his immoral actions, Olaf is not portrayed as a purely evil character. He is shown to have moments of vulnerability and doubt, suggesting that he may have some level of awareness of the wrongness of his actions. Similarly, the Baudelaire children doubt the rightness of their actions as it never leads them happiness and safety. Additionally, his love for his former girlfriend, Kit Snicket, and his desire to reunite with her, show that Olaf is capable of caring for others on some level.

Overall, Count Olaf's and the Baudelaire children's morality in the "Series of Unfortunate Events" is shaped by a complex combination of factors, including his upbringing, personal experiences and the failure of social structures that were supposed to protect them.

Both the antagonist and the protagonists have had their concept of right and wrong influenced by their circumstantial necessities and the socio-political factors that aligned with what they wanted to believe which again is informed by the personal experiences of their life. None of which helped them to really understand what is right and what is wrong. The only thing the opposition between the protagonist and the antagonist, or in the larger scheme of the novels and web series, "those who put out fires" and "those who start fires" suggests an inadequacy of the mold morality is placed in.

In the episode "Penultimate Peril:2," in the courtroom scene, Count Olaf and the Baudelaire children attack this inadequacy head on. The court is filled with people who want to help the Baudelaire children. Count Olaf pleads he is innocent and Baudelaire children are not as innocent as they pretend to be. The Baudelaire children tell them that Olaf is manipulating facts and that the people in the court room will help them prove it. Olaf says,

> Help you? Look around! I see a banker who care more about a promotion than three orphans. I see a man too afraid to protect you and a woman who values paperwork over people's lives. A vice principal who is more than happy to let me in his school as long as I stroked his ego. I see rich people who only cared about you because you were "in," and villagers who only took you in to do your chores. I see volunteers whose complicated codes and pretentious literary references are useless against the real treacheries of the world. And presiding over them all, a justice so blind, she let me marry you. These so-called decent people have done more to help my schemes than any of my associates. They should be up here right now… Because here is the real truth that no one is willing to tell you… there are no noble people in the world.

Olaf claims that he is innocent because despite their actions and intentions, everyone except for Olaf, are called faultless only because they were within the dominant notion of morality. To this the Baudelaire children claim that their parents were noble even if no one else is. Olaf continues to destroy this notion of the children as well by revealing it was their parents' actions that resulted in the series of the unfortunate events. This shift in the debate from morality to noble people is crucial. Olaf's insistence on the non-existence of noble people and the Baudelaires' insistence on their existence reveals a key property of morality. There is a function of meaning that morality performs. It is not understanding itself but a tool that leads to it. What does morality lead to?

Noble people and morality are connected to each other. Not in the sense that they are dependent on each but in the sense that existence of one suggests the existence of other. Noble people are those who are able to embody moral excellence. Noble people are good and they do good. To the Baudelaire children, the existence of noble people is more tangible and the basis of their belief in morality. To Olaf, who sees the myriad ways morality has failed him, believes that morality cannot produce noble people. But if it was just about morality, for either of them, then the debate would have ended with the people in the courtroom whose actions, though adhered to some version of morality, did more harm. They are proof enough that morality doesn't serve any purpose. Why shift the debate to the noble people?

The dilemma may have turned from morality to good people because the concept of "goodness" is often closely tied to morality. Furthermore, the idea of "good people" may be more relatable and concrete than the abstract concept of morality. It's easier for people to understand and relate to the idea of someone being a "good person" than to grapple with complex moral theories. Therefore, morality does not hold any workable meaning by itself as it is very vulnerable. However, it is a tool that leads to meaning with has objective properties, which is not ambiguous, which may not be so easy to tamper with – goodness. The purpose of morality is to help the understand what goodness is, how to maintain it, how to multiply it. If it does not serve that purpose, then it holds no worth. However, this in no way reflects upon goodness.

Count Olaf refrains from killing someone when reasoned to doubt his actions. He saves the love of his life right before he dies. Even the nastiest of characters could not be devoid of some amount of goodness. This reveals one objective quality of goodness that it can be found anywhere. The Baudelaire children where inventors, readers, cooks and they met countless people in their journey who were poets, researchers, judges, teachers, or managers who found goodness in what they did. This reveals that goodness can be shared with what we do. It can be multiplied. All characters in the books and the web series did what they did not because they had to do bad or wanted to do bad (although such people can exist in reality and this an exception, not a norm; and understanding this exception is beyond the scope of this work) but because they thought it was good to do so or because they thought the world was devoid of any goodness and it did not matter what they do. This reveals our relation with goodness. That we would prefer to be informed by it.

I have listed three objective qualities of goodness. No one mind can come close to defining concepts like goodness because they are beyond our limited understanding. A 15 cm scale cannot measure a sky-high pillar. Just like it took countless minds to bring about the understanding of something universal like atoms, concepts like goodness would require similar efforts. These concepts are like the "great unknown" in "A Series of Unfortunate Events." We can encounter it anytime and knowing it entirely may not be possible. However, this is where subjectivity and our personal experiences can come to use.

Subjectivity can help construe anything in any way we want but it can only do so with abstract concepts not with concepts that have objective properties. We will not be able to turn an ice cream into a brick or vice-versa with our subjectivity. Even the most minimum intellectual enquiry into goodness reveals that it has objective properties. Subjectivity can help us bring down goodness to our level of understanding. When we anchor goodness in our experience, we begin to see its many properties.

What we might experience will be different from each other. Sole experiences will reveal different hues of it and not its entirety. Unlike the four blind men who encountered different parts of an elephant and made different conclusions about it, if we bring together our experiences of goodness we might be able to piece it together and reach an understanding. However, if we continue to follow postmodernism emphasis on fragmentation, relativism, and irony, it will only lead to a proliferation of solipsistic and nihilistic tendencies, which ultimately contribute to a loss of meaning and purpose. In this view, postmodernism's critique of grand narratives and foundational truths ultimately led to a dead end, bound us in a loop, where we are not able to find solutions to the problems that the contemporary world faces.

We can continue to let theory inform us that it has all come to an end but either way, cultural artifacts have begun to tell us otherwise.

References:

Snicket, Lemony. *A Series of Unfortunate Events.* HarperCollins Publishers, 1999-2006.

Josephson-Storm, Jason Ananda. *Metamodernism: The Future of Theory.* University of Chicago Press, 2021.

"A Series of Unfortunate Events." *Netflix*, season 1-3, Jan. 2017 -2019.

Jameson, Frederic. "Postmodernism, or the Cultural Logic of Late Capitalism." *Postmodernism: A Reader*, edited by Thomas Docherty, Harvester Wheatsheaf, 1993, pp. 221-239.

www.ingramcontent.com/pod-product-compliance
Lightning Source LLC
LaVergne TN
LVHW021139160826
845679LV00023B/1963

* 9 7 9 8 8 9 4 7 5 4 9 8 7 *